The Practice of the

M000204994

Exploring the unity of the practice of prayer and the practice of theology, this book draws together insights from world-class theologians including Rowan Williams, Andrew Louth, Frances Young, Margaret R. Miles, Sebastian Brock, and Nikolaï Sakharov. Offering glimpses of the prayer-life and witness that undergirds theological endeavour, some authors approach the topic in a deeply personal way while others express the unity of prayer and the theologian in a traditionally scholarly manner. No matter what the denomination of the Christian theologian – Greek or Russian Orthodox, Roman Catholic, Anglican, Methodist – authors demonstrate that the discipline of theology cannot properly be practised apart from the prayer life of the theologian. The prayer of the theologian shapes her or his approach to theology. Whether it be preaching, teaching, writing or research, the deep soundings of prayer inform and embrace all.

Martin Laird, O.S.A., is Professor of Early Christian Studies in the Department of Theology and Religious Studies at Villanova University, USA.

Sheelah Treflé Hidden is a Research Associate with the Heythrop Institute for Religion and Society at Heythrop College, University of London, UK.

The Practice of the Presence of God

Theology as a way of life

**Edited by Martin Laird
and Sheelah Treflé Hidden**

Routledge
Taylor & Francis Group

LONDON AND NEW YORK

First published 2017
by Routledge
2 Park Square, Milton Park, Abingdon, Oxon OX14 4RN

and by Routledge
711 Third Avenue, New York, NY 10017

Routledge is an imprint of the Taylor & Francis Group, an informa business

British Library Cataloguing in Publication Data
A catalogue record for this book is available from the British Library

Library of Congress Cataloguing in Publication Data
Names: Laird, M. S. (Martin S.), editor. | Treflé Hidden, Sheelah, editor.
Title: The practice of the presence of God : theology as a way of life /
edited by Martin Laird and Sheelah Treflé Hidden.
Description: New York : Routledge, 2016. |
Includes bibliographical references and index.
Identifiers: LCCN 2016027667| ISBN 9781472478290 (hardback : alk. paper) |
ISBN 9781472478320 (pbk. : alk. paper) | ISBN 9781315601922 (ebook)
Subjects: LCSH: Prayer–Christianity. | Spiritual life–Christianity. |
Theology, Practical. | Theology.
Classification: LCC BV210.3 .P7324 2016 | DDC 230.023–dc23
LC record available at https://lccn.loc.gov/2016027667

ISBN: 978-1-4724-7829-0 (hbk)
ISBN: 978-1-4724-7832-0 (pbk)
ISBN: 978-1-315-60192-2 (ebk)

Typeset in Bembo
by Out of House Publishing

Contents

PART 3
Theological and liturgical retrievals   61

List of contributors

James Alison is a Roman Catholic theologian and priest. Most noted for his theological application of René Girard's anthropological theory, Alison is the author of many books including *The Joy of Being Wrong, On Being Liked* and *Broken Hearts and New Creations: Intimations of a Great Reversal*.

Sebastian Brock is Emeritus Reader in Syriac Studies at Oxford University. Among his numerous books are *The Luminous Eye: The Spiritual World Vision of St. Ephrem, The Harp of the Spirit: Poems of St. Ephrem* and *The Wisdom of St. Isaac the Syrian*. He also edited *The Hidden Pearl: The Syrian Orthodox Church and its Ancient Aramaic Heritage* (3 volumes) and is co-editor of the recent *Gorgias Encyclopedia of the Syriac Heritage*. He was awarded the Medal of St. Ephrem by His Holiness, Moran Mor Ignatius Zakka I, Patriarch of the Syrian Orthodox Church.

Luigi Gioia, O.S.B., is a Benedictine monk who studied in Italy, France and England. He obtained his doctorate at the University of Oxford with a thesis on St. Augustine's *De trinitate*, recently published by Oxford University Press as *The Theological Epistemology of Augustine's 'De trinitate'*. He is Professor of Systematic Theology at the Pontifical University S. Anselmo, Rome.

Martin Laird, O.S.A., is Professor of Early Christian Studies in the Department of Theology and Religious Studies at Villanova University (USA). His publications include *Gregory of Nyssa and the Grasp of Faith, Into the Silent Land, A Sunlit Absence*, and the forthcoming *An Ocean of Light: Contemplation and the Ethics of Silence*.

Andrew Louth is Professor Emeritus of Patristic and Byzantine Studies at Durham University (UK) and Visiting Professor of Eastern Orthodox Theology at the Amsterdam Centre for Eastern Orthodox Theology (ACEOT). He is also a priest of the Russian Orthodox Diocese of Sourozh (Moscow Patriarchate), serving the parish in Durham.

Margaret R. Miles is the first woman to receive tenure at Harvard Divinity School, where she is Bussey Professor of Theology Emerita as well as Dean Emerita of Graduate Theological Union (Berkeley). Her recent books include

Augustine and the Fundamentalist's Daughter, A Complex Delight: The Secularization of the Breast, 1350–1750 and *Beyond the Centaur: Imagining the Intelligent Body.*

Brian D. Robinette is Associate Professor of Theology at Boston College (USA). He teaches and researches in the areas of systematic and philosophical theology. He is the author of *Grammars of Resurrection: A Christian Theology of Presence and Absence* (Herder & Herder, 2009), which received awards from the Catholic Press Association and the College Theology Society. He is currently working on *The Difference Nothing Makes: Creation, Christ, Contemplation.*

Nikolaï Sakharov, is a monk of the Orthodox Monastery of St. John the Baptist (Essex), which was founded by his great-uncle, Archimandrite Sophrony. His doctoral thesis at the University of Oxford was a study of the theology of Archimandrite Sophrony, which was published in 2002 as *I Love, Therefore I Am.*

Rachel Smith trained as a medievalist at Harvard University. Her research focuses on representations of sanctity in medieval hagiography. She is contributing co-editor of *Hagiography and Religious Truth: Case Studies in the Abramic and Dharmic Traditions* (forthcoming from Bloomsbury Academic) as well as 'Language, Literacy, and the Saintly Body: Cistercian Reading Practices and the *Life of Lutgard of Aywières* (1182–1246)' *The Harvard Theological Review* Fall 2016 and in *The Oxford Handbook of Mystical Theology*. She is Assistant Professor in the Department of Theology and Religious Studies at Villanova University (USA).

Rowan Williams, the 104th Archbishop of Canterbury, is currently Master of Magdalene College, Cambridge University, and Chancellor of the University of South Wales. His numerous publications include *On Augustine; The Edge of Words: God and the Habits of Language, A Silent Action: Engagements with Thomas Merton, Faith in the Public Square, Tokens of Trust: An Introduction to Christian Belief* and *Teresa of Avila.*

Frances Young, is the former Edward Cadbury Professor of Theology at the University of Birmingham, where she also served as Pro Vice-Chancellor. She is a member of the British Academy and the author of many books such as, *From Nicaea to Chalcedon; Brokenness and Blessing: Towards a Biblical Spirituality; Biblical Exegesis and the Formation of Christian Culture; God's Presence: A Contemporary Recapitulation of Early Christianity.*

Preface

The subtitle of this volume, *Theology as a Way of Life*, is not an allusion to Pierre Hadot's famous volume, *Philosophy as a Way of Life*; nor is it intended to be a theological counterpoint or complement to Hadot. However, the *title* of this volume is indeed an explicit reference: *The Practice of the Presence of God* by the Carmelite friar, Brother Lawrence of the Resurrection (1614–1691), whose *lived* theology, whether by working in the kitchen of the French priory where he lived most of his life or by counselling and consoling the many people who sought his counsel over many years.

Title and subtitle together, *The Practice of the Presence of God: Theology as a Way of Life,* intend to express what was simply presumed in the ancient and medieval worlds: there is no goal of life apart from a *way of life* that can lead to that end. Hence, there must be something essential to the practice of theology that can lead to 'theology as a way of life'. That essential 'something' is the role of prayer in the life of the theologian. Only the prayer life of the theologian, the theologian's 'practice of the presence of God' broadly speaking, bears fruit in what can rightly be called 'theology as a way of life'. To this end the chapters that follow address this theme from different perspectives and with varying methodologies and are grouped under the following themes: Foundational Soundings, Personal Accounts of a Theological Life, and Theological and Liturgical Retrievals.

In his brilliant introduction, James Alison states powerfully that the vocation of the theologian is learning to survive without immediate recognition. 'Without a capacity for deferred recognition, there is no theology.' Silence itself, 'the enormous spaciousness that comes from the One for whom death is not an enemy' gives birth to theology. The problem for the theologian is that 'no one rewards silence' or the many years of silence it takes 'to make headway in telling the truth'. In her contribution, Rachel Smith, who makes the case for the continuation of the legacy of St. Anselm in the writings of Hadewijch of Brabant, says, 'theology is not a theorizing that stands at a distance from God, but a relationship that transforms desire and provides the very possibilities of theology'. For St. Anselm and Hadewijch theirs is a 'prayed theology', as Smith puts it, 'a practice of growing into the likeness of God of whom, to whom and in whom one speaks'. Coming from a different angle altogether,

Rowan Williams's contribution brims with all manner of wisdom and insight. He shares similar views with those of Alison and Smith but he solidly grounds theology as a way of life in the very life of the Church (a position with which both Alison and Smith are in accord). 'Theology is, thus, called to repeated conversion; and equally its nature is to call the Church to conversion'. Williams adds further that 'Christian life is itself theological'. Indeed 'To be baptised is to live theologically, to be "in the order of signs"; our calling is to be, in our flesh and blood, a resource by which God's meaning is offered, for healing and for enrichment of a constantly enlarging mind and imagination'. The Russian Orthodox monk, Nikolaï Sakharov, extends what he calls 'the Trinity as our ascetic project' to every corner of society, with special reference (among others) to family life within the Church. Wherever human relationships are found, 'there is a place to practice the Trinity'.

Brian Robinette emphasizes, among other things, the crucial role of contemplative prayer in the practice of theology. Contemplative prayer allows the 'surrendering of the deeply embedded resistances we have towards [our creatureliness]', which is wholly and immediately from God; this constitutes our 'dignity as creatures'. For Robinette, the practice of contemplation leads to the realization that God's transcendence 'is the most immanent reality of our lives, which means that God and creation are "not two"'.

Among the most powerful and poignant contributions to this volume are two personal accounts of theological lives, each by world-renowned professors *emeritae*, Frances Young and Margaret R. Miles. Among all the contributions, theirs are the most direct and personal accounts of how theology has shaped the way they have lived their lives and how their lives have shaped their respective approaches to theology. Frances Young recounts how from childhood her life was imbued with Scripture. Two things stand out during her theological training: patristic exegesis and ecumenical encounters. These, among other life-turning events, have led Young to call herself 'an unconventional Protestant'. While remaining a committed Methodist, over time these ecumenical encounters nurtured both an enlivening sense of communion with other Christian denominations as well as the pain of Eucharistic exclusion by groups she has come to know and love. Margaret R. Miles presents a unique, autobiographical account. She comes to an understanding of her own theological life through dialogue with St. Augustine's *Confessions*, which she has lived with, written about, read and re-read for nearly half a century. At times these respective autobiographers, Miles and Augustine, change places. Miles will use *Confessions* as a mirror and guide in her own life. At other times it seems quite the opposite as Miles's own life interrogates Augustine's and in the process opens great swaths of meaning not often noticed in *Confessions*.

Like Rowan Williams and Nikolaï Sakharov, Andrew Louth also situates the life of prayer in the life of the Church, especially in the Divine Liturgy. Describing the solemn, symbolic, circular movements and rhythms, not only in the Divine Liturgy, but also in the Trinitarian life of God and creation, Louth shifts attention from presence as something one practises to presence as an encounter. While the practice of the Jesus Prayer indeed leads one into the heart of Trinitarian mystery as well as into the heart of the Divine Liturgy, and indeed to all creation, Louth's distinction is an important one, lest one fall into the trap of viewing contemplative practice as a technique to be mastered rather than a skill to prepare one for an encounter of a perpetually flowing Theophany. Louth goes on to suggest that this is the way to understand both the Jesus Prayer and icons: a divine encounter.

Laird explores how Gregory Nazianzen's *Oration* 27 and 28 highlight necessary elements in the formation of the theologian. Both the theologian and the theologian's audience must 'already be living a life that involves the purification/simplification of both body and mind'. Theology takes place in a Church that has been made ready both to speak and listen to theology. Not every occasion is suited to theology, says Gregory. What is the right occasion? Gregory the Theologian says, 'the right occasion is when we possess a vast, inner stillness'.

The famous Syriac scholar, Sebastian Brock, provides us another historical retrieval in the person of St. Ephrem. St. Ephrem expresses his 'prayed theology' in poetry, and Brock, as he has done with the whole of the Syriac tradition over many decades, reveals to the reader the immense beauty and wisdom of this Doctor of the Universal Church on topics ranging from Scripture something living to the nature of creation, life and love. Indeed St. Ephrem's views on the nature of Scripture are worth the price of admission. Brock says, 'for any true *lectio divina* to bear fruit, three things are required: love, purity of heart and right belief'. For St. Ephrem a way of life characterized by these three foundations of Christian living, reveals Scripture in such a way that 'the biblical text becomes like a fountain from which to drink'. As St. Ephrem himself put it in his *Commentary on the Diatessaron I:18*: 'The facets of God's word are more numerous than the faces of those who learn from them ... And God has hidden within his words all sorts of treasures...'. Only a way of Christian living that forms us in such a way as to listen deeply (as distinct from reading critically) to the Silence of the text of Scripture through *lectio divina*, will the living fountain that is Scripture reveal its 'many beauties'.

The theologians invited to contribute to this volume range from among those still young in the cultivation of their theological lives (not their careers) to the majority of the contributors, whose theological lives are well-known, long-established and deeply inspiring by their theological lives that bear fruit time and again in their many contributions to the discipline. They help the rest of us, who seek in the practice of theology something more than a dossier to serve an easily spotted and lamentably frequent theological careerism, but instead seek to cultivate a capacity for deep listening, intellectual humility, wonder and vulnerability through which the Word Incarnate, both in the text of Scripture and in the manifold splendours of tradition, conforms and converts the theologian to a way of life in the life of the Church.

May this volume serve as a nurturing inspiration for the young and as a celebration of the theological lives of those more seasoned in the ways of theology's designs on the theologian.

Martin Laird, O.S.A.
Solemnity of the Birth of St. John the Baptist

Acknowledgements

A large number of essays in this volume are the fruit of a conference held at Heythrop College, University of London, January 2014. Others were solicited because their respective areas of research fit so very well with the theme of the conference. The purpose of the Conference was quite specific: to bring together Christians from Anglican, Orthodox, Protestant and Roman Catholic traditions to address in varying ways how the prayer life of the theologian directly or indirectly addresses theology as a way of life as distinct from theology as a career (distinct should not imply an irresolvable conflict).

Sheelah Treflé Hidden organized the Conference and is indebted to Professor Michael Barnes S.J. and Dr. Michael Kirwan S.J. of Heythrop College, University of London for their unfailing support and counsel in this venture.

Martin Laird, O.S.A., expresses thanks and gratitude to the Master and Fellows of Magdalene College, Cambridge for awarding him a Yip Fellowship in Spring 2015 and for the most warm and gracious welcome; likewise thanks and gratitude to Katholiecke Universiteit Leuven for inviting me as a Visiting Fellow in Fall 2015; special thanks to my academic host Rob Faesen, S.J. Thanks also to Séan O'Dubhghaill for his editorial assistance.

Introduction. Oracles, prophets, and dwellers in silence

Hints of the 'pati divina' in the theology that is being birthed

James Alison

Thank you for inviting me to offer this introductory chapter on the role of prayer in the vocation of the theologian.[1] I have dedicated myself to an essentially classical, almost pre-modern style of theology, as I have followed the thought of the French theoretician of desire, René Girard. Let us start, as of course we should, from where the Sacred Page apparently speaks of our vocation.

It is easy to glide over the first part of 1 Peter 4:11, 'Whoever speaks, as one who utters oracles of God', without having our attention tweaked. In fact, this, from the RSV is a good rendition of the Greek words εἴ τις λαλεῖ, ὡς λόγια θεοῦ. But the word λόγια, very exactly 'oracles', points to a properly mysterious world. Typically we imagine oracles from their pagan sources, like that of Delphos, where the priestess would make mysterious utterances concerning the future. However, in the Hebrew world the words of the prophets are also called 'oracles', by which something very special is understood. Of Moses it is said: ὃς ἐδέξατο λόγια ζῶντα δοῦναι ἡμῖν – 'he received living oracles so as to give them to us'.[2] And of the Jews in general it is said that ἐπιστεύθησαν τὰ λόγια τοῦ θεοῦ – 'to them were entrusted the oracles of God'.[3]

All of which is to say that we are being exhorted, in the Epistle of St. Peter, to something rather more mysterious than right-speaking, or to frequent quotes from the Bible. It is being demanded of us that we dwell within an act of communication that emanates from the Almighty 'in person'.

This is where I would like to begin to think about the vocation of the theologian in emerging circumstances. By referring to 'whoever speaks', the Epistle has in mind those who have received a certain sort of gift. And it is, if you like, the form taken by receiving this gift in our current context, which interests me.

For indeed, every word is situated; it comes from somewhere; it emanates from some human situation. And if God were one of the gods, we could easily understand that God's voice would possess those who might enter into a mystical trance: they would pronounce oracles out of their ecstasy. After all, in animist religions the spirit 'comes down' upon the initiates, and 'moves' them to speak in voices not their own and to say things which apparently do not come from them. The problem is that the gods are projections, functions of the group dynamic. And even though this be not in the initiates intention, the voice which speaks through them is a voice moved by the tensions, desires, rivalries and envies of the group.

God, however, is not one of the gods. One of the ways by which we may understand that the Almighty who speaks is not a voice that emanates from any place within the group dynamic, is not a participant in, or partisan towards, the tensions of those present, is that the Almighty is authentically from elsewhere. However, for it to be authentically from elsewhere, there has to be at least some anthropological basis by which we may detect that it is not part of the group's dynamic, that a word is being addressed to us which does not come, in the last instance, from ourselves. That is to say, the word emanating from God, who is not one of the gods, proffers itself to us, in addition, as a criterion for our own words. To allow this, it has to have something in common with our world formed by words of self-deception and flattery, but without being rooted in the terrain of our mendacity and convenience.

It is from here, it seems to me, that we understand something of the basic scenario from which theology flows. In this basic scenario, there are two contrasting sorts of ground. One, which is stable rock, and the other, which is quicksand. The scenario is that of the Passion, and in terms of structure, it is easy to understand. We're dealing with the more or less accelerated movement of a crowd and of religious and political leaders that we call a lynching. That is to say, where the expulsion of someone held to be a dangerous evildoer is orchestrated, little by little, and without any one person being responsible for it. This act tends to produce a certain peace and unanimity among the participants, who are normally not allies, but, in many cases, have previously been rivals and enemies.

Well, it is not only in the Gospel accounts of the Passion that we find this basic scenario, described with a plethora of details, but also in many other texts, both ancient and modern. Moreover, it is a scenario which, in one form or another, is known to us all, from Incidents (with an upper case I) in the political and social life of our respective countries; from Incidents of genocide, of wars, of social and political movements, to incidents (with a lower case i) in the playgrounds and courtyards of all our schools, convents, seminaries, and so forth. There, where the process of the socialization of adolescents typically advances through learning how to prevent the group finger, which picks out the class fairy, or the group weakling, falling on me.

Now, in this scenario it is typical for the participants to contrast the solid rock of group-belonging with the quicksand within which the castout-du-jour is sinking. Solidity is constructed by the majority opinion, the shared perception, of who the 'good guys' are, and who is the 'bad guy', and why. And insecurity consists in the rapid loss of reputation, of being, of belonging, and in some cases of life itself, undergone by the one upon whom the group finger alights.

Please note that in this scenario there are two voices, two 'words', one might say – two versions. One is waxing strong: the account emanating from the group dynamic as it moves to unanimity against the 'evildoer'. And the other, which is on the wane, emanating, with ever greater weakness and loss of credibility, from the one who is on the way out of being, out of existence. The two voices are absolutely incompatible, for one of them says, with every conceivable social and cultural variant: 'we have a law, and by that law this one must die'. Which is to say: 'All of our movement towards unanimity, and towards the cleansing of our group of whatever contaminates it, comes from God'. And the other voice says: 'they hate me without cause'. Which is to say, 'The whole dynamic which is leading them to expel me is but a lie, and that which seems so stable now is but a fleeting convenience'.

I would like to note here that the sole condition of the possibility of Christian theology is the return, three days after this scenario, of the silenced, dead victim. He reveals himself, with no trace of rancour, and with all the power of one who forgives those who were accomplices to his lynching, to have been the true protagonist of the scene. So, there begins to irrupt into our midst the strange sensation that what had seemed to us to be most solid and dependably from God was nothing more than quicksand, and that all the strength and solidity of the immovable rock has been made present to us in the vulnerability of the despised one.

Now please notice something. For this suggests that there are two ways of being a theologian. One is to summon up, from the sacred texts and the laws and customs of any of our groups, religious justifications for the movement towards group unanimity, by contrast with some evildoer. For this, the only gift that is necessary is that of party spirit. The other way of being a theologian is through the long process of becoming aware that we have been wrong, that I was wrong to make myself an accomplice to the group in my desire to survive the fatal violence that was threatening.

The starting point of Christian theology is that the weak and vulnerable presence of that man who allowed himself to be despised and executed was a dense, powerful and deliberate act of communication, flowing not from some sense of party spirit, but from the Creator of everything that is. That is to say, the voice that authentically comes from elsewhere takes in our midst a very specific form which is both recognizably human, and at the same time, impossible as merely human. This is the act of communication from our victim who has come back among us and is letting us off our participation in the lynching. And this act of communication is not simply a reactive 'pardon'. It reveals itself as the deliberate, creative act of one who entered with knowledge, forethought into our midst, and into that place of shame and humiliation. However, not so as to show us how wicked we are, but rather because he knew that we have such fear of that place of shame, that only by his occupying it, and demonstrating that this place is inhabitable, and not toxic, might we begin to be redirected towards other sorts of social construction. Towards ones that are, in fact, more favourable to our growth, our becoming and our flourishing as human beings.

The starting place of theology, then, is not only the fact of the basic scenario, but the process of our tumbling into awareness that behind the one who occupied the place of the victim with the waning voice, the implausible account and the weak presence, there was a power and a benevolence that were reaching out to us *before we could even begin to imagine them*. The act of communication consisted in occupying that place, which is, in our terms, a non-place, so as to be able, starting from there, to be able to reveal the whole loving-kindness and firmness of the creative power of God.

Well then, if this is true, then the process by which we come to be theologians, those who speak oracles of God, is much more subtle than it might seem. Because our place with relation to the divine voice is not something neutral, objective and clearly detectable by our mere intelligence and fine education. Our place is, if you will, the highly precarious place of those who are beginning to become aware of quite how much we are bound to what seemed strong, but is in fact only fleeting mendacity. It means that the voice which possesses us and allows us to speak is a voice to which we do not have access except in so far as we allow ourselves to be forgiven, deconstructed and recreated. No theological discourse is Christian if it doesn't show its foundation in a process of breaking the heart, made possible by the generosity of the forgiving victim. In other words, the touchstone of all Christian theological discourse is that it is underpinned by the process of the repentance of the one who speaks. In exactly the same way that we are only Church in the degree to which we are learning to leave behind a certain victimary, social formation, so as to enter into a gratuitous one which is born of the generosity of a victim not ourselves.

If, then, the form which is taken by our becoming oracles is the process of being brought to speech as we begin to receive the identity and the voice which emanate from the crucified one, that is, from the 'non-place' within the quicksand of the violent forms of human togetherness, then something similar is true with respect to the possibility that we might become prophets.

It is very traditional to affirm that theology forms part of the spiritual gift of prophecy to which there are several references in the New Testament. And I do not wish in any way at all to diminish that truth. It seems to me, rather, that there are two ways to falsify it: one sins by an excess of modesty, for it considers that the hard reality of institutional classes, Greek grammar tests, examinations in canon law, and extensive knowledge of the philosophical tendencies of the German Enlightenment of yesteryear, sit ill beside the notion that we are doing theology so as to receive with greater rigour the gift of prophecy. This voice says: 'let us be content with small truths, and not aspire too high'. The other sins by an excess of romanticism, for it imagines that the content of prophecy can be given by current patterns of thought, both ideological and combative, more or less easy to digest, which will allow me to be converted into a hero in the eyes of my contemporaries as I seek the martyrial position of being another 'good guy' misunderstood and disdained by the world. This voice says: 'the great truth which I understand gives me permission olympically to ignore the small truths with which the mediocre busy themselves'.

Both excessive modesty and romanticism mislead with respect to the gift of prophecy within which theology is written, for both miss out on what is at its centre: learning to tell the truth. The act of communication that emanates, as we have seen, from the forgiving victim – the gift of prophecy, or speaking from God, has everything to do with telling the truth. It presupposes that the human tendency that affects us all inclines us to convenience, survival and self-flattery rather than to truth. And it offers us a new way of telling the truth: the truth that comes from the victim who is on the way out of the world. Which is to say: starting from its innocence, and its refusal to believe in the reasons which its persecutors give for their hostility to it, starting from its refusal to lay hold of the potential lifebelts thrown in its direction so that it can get on board with them in their analysis of the situation, there is born the possibility of unmasking the lies which abound in the context in which the victim lives.

Now please notice some of the special characteristics of the gift of prophecy born of Christ and of his Spirit. In the first place it suggests that the prophet is not a legislator who dictates the word of God from above, from a position of power disguised as one of neutrality; nor are they a prophet whose ability to foresee the future comes from phantasmagorical supernatural sources. No, the gift of prophecy emanates very strictly from passing slowly and patiently through the process of undergoing potential loss of reputation, of power, of the means of making a living, and even of life itself, for it is better to be dead than to be complicit in the murderous lie. And this process of being stripped of things that are in themselves good, like reputation, ability to make a living, and even life itself, does not happen because I am looking for it, so as to turn me into a hero. It is because I am learning how to love even those who are destroying me, and for that reason, it is worth my while offering them the possibility of recognizing the truth, even if I am not around to see them twig to it, and to witness their change of heart. Starting from this patient process, it is indeed given to the prophet to point towards things that are to come, because the prophet knows the victimary mechanism and its collateral effects from within.

It is here that I would like to insist on something little taught in our theological (and even less in our clerical) formation programmes. Coming to learn to tell the truth in little things is what will allow us one day to remain standing when there comes upon us the temptation to make ourselves accomplices of the lie in something big. If we despise the little steps in learning to tell the truth, telling ourselves 'these are insignificant white lies, of no comparison with what really matters, the grand heroic truth', then the moment of the grand heroic truth will arrive, and we will not even be aware that we are on the other side, persecuting the one who is speaking it. On the contrary, this text is of lifelong importance, 'Whoever is faithful in a very little is faithful also in much; and whoever is dishonest in a very little is dishonest also in much.'[4]

I would like to propose a different model for learning to tell the truth from the one that is usual in our discipline, let alone Roman Catholic church structures. What is normal in those contexts is a paradigm of truth-telling coming from two main sources: philosophical thought of a Cartesian stripe seeking certainties held together within a logical system. A clear example of this is seen in the neo-scholastic formation of a certain generation of many Roman Catholic theologians. The second source is the mentality derived from a Salamantine legal education, among others, one widely diffused through all the disciplines to be learnt throughout the Spanish-speaking world.[5] This latter puts enormous emphasis on learning by rote big chunks of text, of theses, and of magisterial formulations, so as to be able to repeat them verbatim whether in examinations, or in everyday life.

Well, I want to make it quite clear that I have nothing at all against either certainty, or logic, or formulations or exercises of memory. However, it seems to me that as prototypes of truth-telling these paradigms are inadequate. From the seventeenth century up until the present, in the same period as the philosophical and notarial forms that I have mentioned were being forged, there was also developing, but as if hidden from the gaze of theology, another discourse, another way of telling the truth. A discourse, which has given many people magnificent resources for truth-telling. This discipline is that of the novel. Starting with Cervantes and Shakespeare, and moving through the great authors of the nineteenth and twentieth centuries such as Stendhal, Proust and Dostoyevsky, and so to our contemporaries, another, very distinctive and important mode of truth-telling has been brought to light. A mode which should not be despised by those who wish to be good exponents of sacred texts but also have much more in common with narratives than they do with philosophical or legal texts.

The pillars of this narrative tradition, whose peaks are Cervantes and Dostoyevsky, have, I would say, something in common. They allow there to be glimpsed, maybe over the course of various novels, traces of penitent autobiography dressed in borrowed garments. Typically they are novels written by authors whose own exceedingly painful process of discovering themselves to have been living a lie, a lie built up by the desires of the group, and one to which they had considered themselves immune, leads them to a profound loss of being, and then to a re-discovery of their social group starting from a new 'I', born from the ruins of their previous identity. The excellence of the novels in question is recognized in the capacity of their readers to discover that the story they are being told is their own story, told with a far greater scope and dimensions than they might have suspected, and taking them to an understanding of who they are that they hadn't imagined. In other words, they recognize that they are being told the truth about themselves, unflattering though that experience may be.

This, at last, seems to me to be a properly prophetic dimension of the theology that is being birthed, and one we have to re-evaluate. If we are going to be truth-tellers who are learning to tell the truth through having discovered ourselves as liars, people caught up in all sorts of mendacity and violence, then we have to learn more than the grammar of theology, which will indeed take us through well-defined institutional phases, ones which may well be clothed in elements of philosophy, of ancient languages, and of legal thinking. In addition to this we will have to learn how to be revisionist autobiographical authors, constantly learning to leave behind those convenient stories of 'hero' or 'victim' that flatter our ego, so as to stumble into a loss of identity before the one who is our victim, but who is offering us the possibility of a new, and unending life story.

Now this process of the loss of group identity, and of the reception of a new identity that flows from the 'non-place', along with the possibility of beginning to speak in the voice of the one who suffered (and not in our own voice, feeling ourselves to be victims) is not a pleasant process. It is a very painful process, which is not to be sought out, but to be received as it comes upon us. It means that, instead of talking from *our* truth, built on foundations of shifting sand, we are beginning to give voice to the Other whose love is communicated through us. And this is a process that doesn't depend on us, but on the true rock, which is transforming this liar into a tiny particle of its own radiance.

Here I fear that I will have to say something rather unpopular, for we are inclined to become tireless parrots of chatty theological verborrhea. But this process of letting go of being the bearers of group values and desires so as to become a theologian, is a process bathed in silence, the silence of one who does not know how to speak. The silence of those who have been caught out in an act of false witness, and who know that their only way out is to go back over their story so as to learn to articulate the non-official version, the inconvenient one in which the wrinkles haven't been ironed out, nor the shortcuts painted over. And for this I need a good chunk of time in which I don't say anything, and in which I pray hard to receive the light of the truth concerning what was really going on in my life. Where I have to learn to prefer the truth that comes from the Other to every lure from a more comfortable truth.

The problem is this: No one rewards silence. Rapid response is prized; the one with sure-footed opinions or ready answers in a stormy situation is respected. There is no reward for the months and years of silence necessary for us to give up lying and make headway in telling the truth. However, that silence, and the non-reactive capacity to tell the truth with no concern for convenience, is worth much, much more than what any of us could earn by saying a lot with very little background silence. And this means that an essential part of the shape of how we receive a theologian's vocation is learning to survive without immediate recognition. In other words, without a capacity for deferred recognition, there is no theology. And that means that without the poverty that goes along with being someone who doesn't have anything immediately useful to offer, there is no theology.

The silence which gives birth to theology is the enormous spaciousness that comes from the One for whom death is not an enemy; the One who is giving us time to reconstruct true life stories, who does not seek to humiliate us, nor that we humiliate others. It is the spaciousness of the One for whom time floats peacefully and with unconcern on sparks of eternity. Let us learn to delight in it.

Notes

1 This chapter is a revised version of a presentation to the First International Congress of Theology Students, Pontificia Universidad Javeriana, Bogotá, Colombia (eds). Translated by the author.
2 Acts 7:38.
3 Romans 3:2.
4 Luke 16:10.
5 From the fifteenth to the eighteenth century the Law School of the University of Salamanca (along with that of Alcalá) provided the bureaucracy of the Spanish Empire.

Part 1
Foundational soundings

1 Theology as a way of life

Rowan Williams

1.

Theology is what we call any serious attempt to represent and explore the meanings of the word 'God', which is presumably what Wittgenstein meant in his throwaway remark that theology was a kind of 'grammar'.[1] 'Grammar' (he has just said) tells us what sort of object we are talking about, it has to do with the 'essence' of a subject of discourse. And so it entails following out – for example – what sort of criteria are being used to make sure two people are talking about the same thing. Any grammatical study will involve looking hard at how usages of words are established, refined, modified, narrowed or broadened, how a recognizable shared use comes into focus. So, if theology is grammar, it is not going to be able to get away from narratives. This is not to say that the only proper kind of theological talk is story-telling, as some have over-enthusiastically claimed – only that exploring what theological language means obliges us to look and listen.[2] At the beginning of his *Summa theologiae*,[3] Thomas Aquinas argues that 'sacred teaching' can and should be treated as an ordered body of knowledge, a science, but one that arises out of scriptural narrative: it does not deal primarily with narrative, but narrative is what establishes why and how we should rely on 'those through whom God's revelation comes to us'.

Theology, then, is an ordered style of reflection and discovery, a putting in order of what we have come to know, grounded in the inspection and inter-rogation of ways of life, practices. Where and how do people claim to know God, in what circumstances do they say that they have discovered something or that something has been shown to them? It is inseparable from events in which human understanding and capacity somehow 'move on', grow and shift. To take the obvious analogy, musicology is not a series of descriptions of concerts, but actual practices, shifts in perception, shifts in what is possible or thinkable for a practising musician or a whole culture of practising musicians, innovations in performance and analytic description of performance, the technological devel-opment of instruments – all of this is what grounds musicology as science. You can discuss a piece of composition in terms of its patterns and 'values', but what makes such a discussion possible is this cluster of happenings and movements and changes which constitutes musical knowledge in action. And just as with music we are talking about a coming-to-know that is inseparably to do with both mental and bodily happening, so with theology: we are not examining intellectual history alone but that kind of making sense that goes on in material life (and thus also historical and communal life) as well as the analysis of ideas.

When we say that composers 'solve a problem' in their work, we don't mean that they come up with a formula to answer a question, but that they identify the actions that will resolve a clash or collision of sound. And in theology we could speak of 'solving problems' not simply as a clarifying of concepts, but as the process in which concepts are brought into clearer focus through reflection on what practitioners do. In so many theological controversies across the centuries, we can see the circulating relationship between liturgical and sacramental practice and the formulation of ideas – a theological development being promoted on the grounds of doing better justice to the language of the liturgy, a liturgical practice being criticized because of a sharper focus on certain conceptual issues and perhaps ruled out precisely because of its ability to prompt faulty theology.[4]

An observer external to the life of religious communities would be in a position to see something of how these relations worked – would indeed be in a position, sometimes, to trace or at least suggest connections that 'insiders' might miss, often to the embarrassment of the latter. Does such and such a doctrinal idiom imply a practice of authority that silences women? Does a particular devotional habit make it easier to articulate a theological rationale for slavery or absolute monarchy? A good theologian, precisely because such a person is committed to understanding the interaction of practice and doctrine, will not simply deny or ignore this hermeneutic of suspicion. However, what distinguishes the theologian as such from the expert analyst of the habits of religious practitioners is that the theologian begins from within a community *wanting to know more of how it knows God*. For the theologian, the task is not only about 'representing and exploring' what 'God' means, it is also about the representation and exploration of the self.

How do I, how do we, come to the point of claiming to know? Dealing with that question is what makes theology inexorably a matter of self-knowledge – in a way that is not true for the phenomenologist of religion observing what people of faith do. And if I am examining what has made a conviction possible and plausible for me and for us, it becomes imperative to test what we say about ourselves for arbitrary or self-serving elements. We may never arrive at a genuinely detached account of who we are and how we learn, but we can at least develop habits that will make it more possible to see where we *think* we have learned, but have actually projected our needs and worked to their agenda.

At this level, theology is always bound up with the practice of repentance, in the sense that the theologian, in seeking to check such illusions about the process of learning and to identify those false representations of God which turn out to be self-serving, must be deeply attentive to his or her own history – to a particular relation to the past, to the community and its language, to the body in its gendered, mortal, socially constrained character, and to other bodies similarly configured. The theologian is committed to self-awareness, consciousness of limits and consciousness of the pitfalls of self-representation. That is why theology classically insists so much on the receptive and contemplative dimension. The practice of theology as a way of life moves in and out of silence and in and out of intense self-scrutiny; not in order to produce an anxious perfectionism, but so as to rein in the confident speculative spirit that will so readily assume we can 'know' God without changing our fundamental spiritual attitudes. And in this connection, it needs to be said that a 'theological life' or a 'theological event' may be something that occurs in all sorts of contexts well outside the limits of what most would call professional theology. It is in this sense, that Jon Sobrino, for example, can speak of the life and martyrdom of Archbishop Oscar Romero of El Salvador as a 'theological event'[5] – a series of happenings in which the Word of God and the language of human suffering come together as an inseparable event of meaning in the world, and in which the simply personal vision or thought of the preacher or theologian recede. One might equally well say of the life of any saint, in fact, that it is a theological event, where human acting and receiving become a manifestation of divine meaning or purpose and thus bring decisive change into the world.

2.

Theology as a way of life, therefore, involves at least three significant elements. It must be accompanied by a real growth in 'literacy' about oneself – a willingness to recognize the patterns of desire and imagination which, for good or ill, shape what is said. It must be marked by a profound patience with what *resists* being said, a patience both with my own inarticulacy and with the stumbling articulation of those with whom I am speaking. And it must, therefore, be committed to a conversational engagement with others seeking the same level of meaning, an openness to the discernment of others inside and outside the community (because not everyone who seeks this level of meaning, the level at which God's purposes and human speech and action coincide, will automatically share the same believing vocabulary).

   To say this should not imply that all theological activity *reduces* to penitence, self-examination, silence and the invitation to shared discernment; there are contexts in which it is right and necessary to affirm, to take the risk of 'staking' the truth (however imperfect) of a doctrine or perception. Theology includes, crucially, the doxological and liturgical function, which is as much a feature of this 'way of life' as any amount of scrutiny and reticence. But it remains true that a doxological theology which is not critically aware of its own fragile position – like the hazelnut in the hands of Christ in Julian of Norwich's 'showing', fragile and tiny but ultimately secure as an object of love – will be liable to distortion; it may become what Luther castigated as a 'theology of glory', an assertion of the triumph of the theologizing mind as opposed to the theology of the cross which is drawn back to dispossession. And for an entire community to be practising theology is for it to be practising a theologically informed worship which leads both to individual self-examination and to shared reflection; all of it, within the context of a worshipping practice which is 'theological', because it takes it for granted that it celebrates and enacts a state of affairs not brought about by human words or actions.

This reminds us that the reason we do theology at all is precisely that a state of affairs has been brought about that is surprising – new, unmerited, dispro-portionate to any effort of ours. In living theologically, we seek to enlarge our minds and hearts a little further towards the dimension of this new state of affairs – recognizing, of course, that we shall never arrive at a full correspond-ence with it, since this new state of affairs is, ultimately, a divine state of affairs, 'how it is with God'. What is new, in the language of Christian Scripture, is that we are set free to address God and to relate to God in the same way that Jesus did (and does). Our new state of affairs is 'filiation', the condition of being made a son or daughter of the Father of Jesus; this is what is indentified by the New Testament writers as the fresh and distinctive thing which marks out the com-munity of believers, the corporate Body of Christ. The God we are seeking to talk about is a God who characteristically *adopts*, who gratuitously welcomes all comers into the place eternally occupied by the Word or Son. In other words, this is a God who is known as someone who can be addressed in a certain way – known in the second rather than the third person. A theology, a reflec-tion that seeks to clarify the 'grammar' of such a God, is necessarily embedded in 'second-person' practices. In seeking to know better how it knows God, it acknowledges that God is known in the gift and process of adoption and in growth in that relation. As such, it is nourished by two fundamental moments – a divine act of welcome that springs us from the traps of self and a continuing divine act of 'acclimatization' or 'assimilation' that establishes our new identity as related in this particular way to the Father of Jesus. And if that is the case, the test of an authentic and effective theology is the degree to which it represents and opens up to these aspects of divine action.

Hence, once again, the need for a theological way of life to be poised between penitence and wonder, and for a theological language to point to these two moments. A language and practice that is transparent to the divine action that creates the state of affairs we have identified will be marked by a consciousness of its own riskiness and by its ability to celebrate its receptive character by both praise and silence. It will acknowledge how readily it can slip back into the world of the self and its comforts, into a state of affairs that is not 'how it is with God', and so will be manifestly concerned to declare its modest aims and to apply itself to challenging idolatries. But it will also be working to generate ways of speaking that are directed into the abundance of divine life – and to resist formulations that narrow the scope of what can be affirmed of divine life. The point of identifying a discourse as 'heretical' – which is not a quaint archaism, as Christian dissidents in Nazi Germany or apartheid in South Africa have recognized – is to name certain kinds of theologizing as inadmis-sible because they say less than they should about God's own freedom (thus, we resist reductionist models of Christology which deny the radical inseparability of divine and human act in Jesus or monistic pictures of God which deny the eternity of gift and reciprocity in divine life) or about God's freedom to deal justly and mercifully with all human creatures (thus resisting racial mythologies and gender inequalities).

But the more important aspect, which we mentioned at the outset, is the generation of ways of speaking about divine abundance; indeed, it could be said that where this is properly alive, the risk of one or another kind of heresy is diminished. Theology serves liturgy, as it is itself served and shaped *by* liturgy. If the central movement of liturgy is articulating and opening up to the foundational fact of the new life, the new creation, it will be the context in which language about how Christ comes fully alive in person and community as the eternal prayer to the Father takes place in our human midst. What theology undertakes to do is to test and explore such language, teasing out implications, identifying distorting or trivializing usages, clearing the way to more honest celebration.[6] It will have done its job if it helps towards a more lucid heart and mind – a heart accepting of its own deceit and weakness and not despairing, turning in wonder to what transforms and frees it.

'Theology as a way of life' is, ultimately and simply, an aspect of the life of 'filiation' as it becomes aware of itself. The believer begins from a grateful conviction that the state of affairs in which he or she stands is new and in some sense free from the conditioning of the past; the words in which this is embodied from the very first moment are the words of Christ-formed prayer to the Father. The shape of our liberation is that we are delivered from the anxiety of placating God into a liberty in which we can both acknowledge our untruthfulness and open ourselves to an undefeated divine truth which works for our healing. In briefer and more concentrated terms, the shape of our liberation is that we become – as some teachers describe it – a place where Christ happens. Theology seeks to find words that affirm and give thanks aptly for this; and also to find words that check and question the temptations to self-reliance and complacency that arise in the theological enterprise. It is a way of life that is shaped daily by 'eucharist' in the widest possible sense: thanksgiving, but most specifically the thanksgiving that allows itself to become transparent to the Giver, as in the Eucharistic action of the liturgy itself. The great Jesuit theologian, Maurice de la Taille,[7] famously said that at the Last Supper Jesus 'placed himself in the order of signs'. We might paraphrase this by saying that in the Supper Jesus, who is himself the paradigm of 'theological event', in which human word and action become the embodiment of divine action, creates a theological event in which others can participate. He creates a language, a sign-system, which grounds and unites a 'theological' community, the community in which transformation continues through repentance and praise and ceaseless exploration of the meaning established in the fleshly life and death and resurrection of the Word of God. The particular work we name as theology is where this continuous transformation deliberately labours towards fuller awareness of itself, towards a 'grammar', to pick up again the language with which we started. It is the labour of discerning better the essence of the divine action as it has reached us, the act by which we are made children of God – and thus also the essence of healed human nature.

Theology is, thus, called to repeated conversion; and equally its nature is to call the Church to conversion. It is in this sense that the sacraments are central to the theological enterprise, and that the Church's ministry is characteristically theological (and not limited by mere function). Theology is emphatically a way of life for the ordained. But the implication of all that has been said here is, of course, that Christian life is itself theological, the event of convergence between divine act and human communication, even (paradoxically) when that convergence is expressed in recognition of the infinite gulf between human speaking and divine acting. To be baptized *is* to live theologically, to be 'in the order of signs'; our calling is to be, in our flesh and blood, part of the resource by which God's meaning is offered, for healing and for the enrichment of a constantly enlarging mind and imagination.

Notes

1 Ludwig Wittgenstein, *Philosophical Investigations*, 3rd edition (Oxford: Blackwell, 2001), p. 99.
2 A sharp critical analysis of loose talk about narrative theology can be found in Francesca Aran Murphy, *God is Not a Story: Realism Revisited* (Oxford: Oxford University Press, 2007).
3 I.1.ii ('Whether sacred teaching is a science').
4 Examples abound. In early Christianity, the question of what was actually happening in the Eucharist clearly affected what was thought to be defensible doctrine; at the Reformation, what many saw as corrupt practice was reformed in order to avoid inconsistent or 'superstitious' teaching; in the wake of Vatican II, there were controversies over whether the liturgical practice of Benediction of the Blessed Sacrament was to blame for a 'commodified' or static theology of Eucharistic presence.
5 Jon Sobrino, *Archbishop Romero: Memories and Reflections*, 2nd edition (Eugene, OR: Wipf and Stock, 2004), pp. 168–74.
6 On the theme of theology and honesty, see the outstanding work of Andrew Shanks, especially *Faith in Honesty: the Essential Nature of Theology* (London: Ashgate, 2005).
7 See the fine recent monograph by Michon M. Matthiesen, *Sacrifice as Gift: Eucharist, Grace and Contemplative Prayer in Maurice de la Taille* (Washington DC: Catholic University of America Press, 2013), especially p. 290, n.3.

2 Undergoing something from nothing

The doctrine of creation as contemplative insight

Brian D. Robinette

1. Systematic theology and the way of unknowing

As a systematic theologian, I am sometimes achingly aware of the gulf that can separate the work of theology from the lived reality of Christian faith. Not that systematic theology as such warrants this charge, but the perception that it does is not uncommon, and there are more than a few examples that lend support to that perception. Often enough, this (real or perceived) gulf is characterized by the disconnect between doctrinal reflection and lived experience – or just as likely, by the disjunction between conceptually driven 'theology' and affectively embodied 'spirituality'.

I am also aware of various objections to systematic theology that characterize it as anachronistic or, worse, a brand of 'totalizing' thinking that represses or distorts lived reality in some way. Notwithstanding the fact that systematic theology today appears to be in what Sarah Coakley calls 'a remarkable state of regeneration', a number of common objections to this style of theology – and perhaps to theology more generally – can be cited.[1] Coakley herself points to three. The first is that systematic theology is a form of 'onto-theology' that lays claim to comprehending God within a system of references, as though God were a kind of 'object' in the world we might grasp or at least extrapolate on the basis of immanent causes and universal principles. The second is related to the first, but points to the political implications of a form of discourse that, because it aims for systematic clarity in relating various features of Christian faith in a coherent and compelling way, results in the suppression of marginalized voices and cultural perspectives that would otherwise disrupt its predilection for order. In short, systematic theology tends towards 'hegemony'. The third objection, according to Coakley, assumes a particular feminist and psychoanalytic critique that regards systematic theology as a typically 'male' enterprise that seeks to control and master, and which represses or at least subordinates those aspects of life associated with embodiment, affectivity, and the unconscious.

Coakley's own effort in systematic theology, which she describes as the 'attempt to provide a coherent, and alluring, vision of the Christian faith', seeks to meet each of these objections, and in the first instalment of her multivolume project (the only volume published to date) she does so by working through the doctrine of the Trinity.[2] It is an ambitious and exciting project that will be the subject of lively conversation and debate for years to come as new volumes appear. What I find especially striking about her effort, which I intend to develop in my own way here, is her consistent appeal to the ascetico-contemplative life in the work of theology, or what elsewhere she calls its 'contemplative matrix'.[3]

Systematic theology, in this view, is emphatically not the effort to build a towering, windowless edifice of interlocking propositions that render God and the Christian life a matter of full comprehension. Neither is its aim for clarity and coherence at odds with a patient sensitivity to lived experience, to the ambiguities and conflicts of interpretation, to the refractoriness of suffering, and to the limits of human knowing. In fact, rightly approached – or better, when lived into – the work of theology is a self-involving risk undertaken from within a living, breathing community, amongst diverse voices and cultural perspectives, and presupposing of a 'way of life' orientated toward that inexhaustible mystery we call 'God'. Theology is an ascetical and contemplative endeavour, not merely an intellectual one. 'It must involve the stuff of learned bodily enactment, sweated out painfully over months and years, in duress, in discomfort, in bewilderment, as well as in joy and dawning recognition'.[4]

As unlikely as it may seem to those who find systematic theology objectionable for one or more of the above reasons, such a discipline is in fact an ascetico-contemplative undertaking that *knows by unknowing*, or as Coakley puts it, proceeds by way of skilful 'un-mastery'.

> For the very act of contemplation – repeated, lived, embodied, suffered – is an act that, by grace, and over time, inculcates mental patterns of 'un-mastery', welcomes the dark realm of the unconscious, opens up a radical attention to the 'other', and instigates an acute awareness of the messy entanglement of sexual desires and desire for God. The vertiginous freefall of contemplation, then, is not only the means by which a disciplined form of unknowing makes way for a new and deeper knowledge-beyond-knowledge; it is also … the necessary accompanying practice of a theology committed to ascetic transformation.[5]

It must be said that this view of theology is not exactly new. Though the inclusion of the social sciences and other forms of critical theory does in fact reflect a way of doing theology that opens up new and challenging frontiers, the foregrounding of contemplation in its elaboration is actually to reclaim the way theology was typically practised throughout the patristic and medieval eras. Not that all theology ceased to exhibit this contemplative dimension with the rise of modernity, but it is nevertheless true that only in recent centuries has the 'scientific' character of theology shifted in such a way that scripture, creeds, and doctrines might be regarded as an independent body of propositions to which one might intellectually assent, rather than pointers to and resources for an array of virtues and habits of mind enacted in daily life.[6] A similar shift is evident in the history of philosophy as well, as Pierre Hadot has shown, with the effect that pre-modern philosophy is typically read today for its doctrinal or argumentative content to the near exclusion of the art of living it advocates, or what Hadot describes as its 'way of life'.[7]

While much more could be said about the shifting senses of theology as a 'scientific' discipline – shifts that have contributed to the modern disciplinary distinctions between 'theology' and 'spirituality' – the main point I wish to emphasize here, in light of Coakley's comments, is that systematic theology, when done well, approaches the 'unknowability' of God by way of practical inhabitation, i.e., as a reality to be *lived into* by grace, by participation, and through a never-ending movement of purgation and transformation lured on by God's inexhaustible self-giving. Such an approach will be different from mere talk *about* God's unknowability. For while it is fashionable today to invoke apophatic styles of theology when stressing the limits of human knowledge, or when characterizing human language as the destabilizing deferral of meaning, a contemplative theology within the Christian tradition will emphasize apophasis as an embodied and communal practice with a Trinitarian shape. 'For contemplation is the unique, and wholly *sui generis*, task of seeking to know, and speak of God, unknowingly; as Christian contemplation, it is also the necessarily bodily practice of dispossession, humility, and effacement which, in the Spirit, causes us to learn incarnationally, and only so, the royal way of the Son to the Father'.[8]

2.   On not being 'two': Discovering *creatio ex nihilo*

I would like to develop further these richly programmatic considerations by turning our attention to another major doctrine within the Christian tradition, namely, the doctrine of creation, in order to show how theological reflection and contemplation are of a piece. In particular, I wish to take up the doctrine of *creatio ex nihilo*, or 'creation from nothing', as an instance in which a seemingly abstract (and recently contested) doctrine gains a far richer significance when approached as the fruit of contemplative insight, which it also informs and helps to guide. In other words, there is, or at least there ought to be, a mutually informing influence between doctrinal reflection and contemplative inquiry in the work of theology; and unless this mutually informing influence is made explicit, a doctrine like *creatio ex nihilo* will likely fall prey to the kind of previously cited objections levelled at systematic theology in general.

If I may put the matter succinctly, *creatio ex nihilo* should not be seen as one among many competing proposals for describing how the universe first began, which is how it is sometimes depicted. Nor should it be regarded as nervously defending God's 'power', or 'divine omnipotence', which is what some critics charge it as doing.[9] Rather, we should see in this doctrine a remarkable invitation: an invitation to discover something about our creatureliness, a discovery that, while richly affirmative and worthy of expression and rigorous thought, cannot be captured in a proposition or come under the domain of comprehension without losing what is essential to it. It refers us to the inexhaustible mystery of our being at all – to the sheer gratuity of existence as such – and does so by drawing us into a skilful 'unknowing', or a deep 'relaxation' into our creatureliness that allows us to accept our contingency and fragility with gratitude and love. *Creatio ex nihilo* names our deepest vulnerability as creatures, which is that we are utterly dependent for our being – that we do not exist from ourselves, but from an unfathomable, yet intimate Other – and it does so by also naming the reason why we can say 'yes' to that dependency without restraint, without fear, without resentment, and without loss of our inviolable dignity as creatures.

In order to see how this might be the case, and how such acceptance is in fact an ongoing process of discovery, it would be useful to explain why *creatio ex nihilo* came to be formulated in the way it did during the second and third centuries. A textbook summary will typically highlight two basic features. The first is that 'creation from nothing' rapidly became the default theological response to a widespread philosophical position that assumed the co-eternity of matter with God. Only God is eternal, so the theological response goes, and God's creative act is without any condition whatsoever. In contrast to a world view in which God imposes forms out of pre-existent materials, or establishes order from a primordial chaos that harbours a range of potencies within it, the creator God who is revealed in the scriptures, and especially the God who raised Jesus from the non-being of death, summons forth all things with a creative liberty that is not conditioned by anything at all. The creator God is not like a demiurge who works within pre-given constraints, and neither is there an external reason or ulterior motive for God's creative act. God is not compelled by some lack, loneliness, or inner agitation to give being to that which is 'other' than God. Indeed, the world does not have to be at all, and yet it is – 'from nothing', which is to say, out of the sheer gratuity of God, upon whom all things continuously depend for their existence.

The second major feature of the doctrine was prompted by various 'gnostic' strains in antiquity that tended to regard matter as the seedbed of evil, and therefore something to be transcended in the quest for salvation. By contrast, *creatio ex nihilo* affirms the original goodness of the world, despite its 'fallen' state, and declares that material reality is the gift of difference, of finitude, given by a loving God who redeems and promises to transfigure eternally the whole of creation for its deification. Material reality is not a barrier to God, as dualistic portrayals of the God–world relation suppose, but the very means by which creatures are united with God. Perhaps this last point is not readily gleaned from the doctrine's name – what does 'from nothing' have to do with the creature's union with God? – but this soteriological interest was in fact a central motivation for theologians like Tatian, Theophilus, Irenaeus, and Tertullian, who together had a significant hand in shaping it. As Gerhard May says of Irenaeus' entire approach to the subject: 'The meaning and nature of the creation are to be understood only in connection with the universal economy of salvation'.[10]

The meaning of *creatio ex nihilo* bears upon much of Christian theology – the doctrine of God, the human person, Christ, salvation, eschatology, etc. – and so it is easy to see why a theologian might wish to elaborate its internal consistency with other major *loci* of the faith. The doctrine of creation might even be seen as establishing something like a grammatical principle that helps to give Christian discourse and imagination a particular shape. By affirming creation as utterly dependent upon God for its existence, and therefore God as radically free in summoning it forth, a fundamental 'distinction' between God and world is named that highlights for us their 'non-competitive' relationship.[11] 'God' and 'world' are not rivals, as though vying for the same 'space' in the exercise of freedom. Though it is common enough for us to imagine God as *a* being among other beings, perhaps even a very big or supreme being who sets all things in motion and who subsequently exercises control over them, thinking this way only situates God within a larger frame of reference and nexus of causes. God would then become a function *within* the world, a causal link within a chain of events, rather than the inexhaustible source and ground *of* the world. As David Bentley Hart puts it, *creatio ex nihilo* affirms that God is

> the creator of all things not as the first temporal agent in cosmic history ... but as the eternal reality in which 'all things live, and move, and have their being', present in all things as the actuality of all actualities, transcendent of all things as the changeless source from which all actuality flows. It is only when one properly understands this distinction that one can also understand what the contingency of created things might tell us about who and what God is.[12]

This last point is crucial: it recalls my earlier insistence that *creatio ex nihilo* is an invitation to discover the deeper significance of our creatureliness. God is 'wholly Other', or radically transcendent, and because of this is also radically intimate to creation. God's 'otherness' is not set apart from the world in an oppositional way, as though occupying an unimaginably distant space. Rather, God's 'otherness' is utterly near and intimate to the creature – nearer to us than we are to ourselves, as Saint Augustine puts it – and thus present to all things as their abiding source and ground. We cannot oppose God's transcendence with God's immanence, for doing so only casts God as a kind of 'object' set apart from, and ultimately in rivalry with, the world. In order to highlight this point, Nicholas of Cusa refers, somewhat paradoxically, to God's 'otherness' as the *non aliud*, the 'not-other'. This phrase reminds us that God's difference from the world cannot be regarded as a separation from the world. On the contrary, precisely because God establishes the world 'from nothing', God is inmost to all things. Karl Rahner puts it this way: 'The difference between God and the world is of such a nature that God establishes and *is* the difference from the world from himself, and for that reason he establishes the closest unity precisely in the differentiation'.[13]

Unity *in* difference: this way of putting it emphasizes that God and world are not to be identified, as a pantheistic outlook would have it. By saying that God is the inmost reality of creation, there is no question of God residing 'inside' the creature in any spatial sense. Neither are God and creation somehow fused or woven together. God truly remains transcendent to creation, and infinitely so, but this is precisely what allows God to be incomprehensibly close to the creature. God 'is not "close" to us, he is the closeness itself', writes Thomas Halík.

> We can still see close objects, but we cannot see closeness itself. We see objects in light—we do not see light itself. If we do not even see our own faces, but only see their reverse reflection in a mirror ... how could we possibly see the face of God?[14]

This last statement already suggests that a contemplative approach will be helpful in appreciating the 'non-objectness' of God, but we should make one more observation before seeing how. If God and world cannot be identified, or imagined as coextensive with one another; and if, as must also be pointed out, God's transcendence means that creation is not an 'extension' of God, or a temporal odyssey that God must undergo in order to be God, then neither can we say that God and world are itemizable realities standing alongside one another. It is not as though we have 'God-plus-world', insists David Burrell, for any attempt to characterize divinity in terms of '*other than* the world' risks incoherence for the way it construes God's transcendence in terms that are negatively defined *by* the world. To speak of God in this way may *seem* like it's emphasizing God's transcendence, but in fact it is limiting that transcendence by defining it in contrast with creation, as if God were displaced by the world.[15] Herbert McCabe makes the same point with his typical clarity and wit: 'It is not possible that God and the universe should add up to make two'.[16] God and world are not 'one', but neither are they 'two'. They are 'not two', or 'non-dual'. Since God is not a creature, not even a very big and magnificent one, God cannot be properly thought of as alongside, inside, or above the world in any spatial sense. While it might seem easy to imagine divine transcendence in just this way, as somehow 'out there' or 'beyond' the furthest reaches of the physical universe, we must eventually subject our imagination to scrutiny and free it from its reifying tendencies. This is not to deny the important role of imagination or conceptualization in the life of faith – Christianity is nothing if not 'incarnational' in sensibility, which means that it affirms the full range of our creatureliness, including the perceptual and affective bases of acting and knowing God – but our imagination and conceptualization must also be purged of any objectifying tendencies that would domesticate the mystery of God, and therefore the mystery of own creatureliness.

3.   Undergoing something from nothing

The question I pose now is whether there is an embodied practice that enables us to gain a richer sense, a lived sense, of what being a creature 'from nothing' might mean. In other words, how do we avoid the potential problem that we are trapped in a conceptual shell game? Given that we have reached the point of multiplying negative statements that insist upon the God–world relation as 'not one' and 'not two', or alternatively, 'non-dual', might we only be more subtly, but still effectively, committed to a conceptual strategy that, however suggestive or rhetorically playful, involves us in an exhausting reliance upon conceptual representations of God after all?

But perhaps this conceptual impasse points to a threshold. Perhaps it is a doorway, rather than an enclosure, and indicative of another mode of inquiry that, while not at all opposed to words or concepts, is not restricted by them either. And perhaps this mode of inquiry is an invitation to further formation, to a process of training (or *askesis*) that can help us cultivate dispositions and habits of mind that purge us from our tendency to regard God as a kind of 'object' in our speech and imagination. If so, such inquiry would likely involve inculcating mental patterns of 'un-mastery', to recall Coakley's phrase, that draw us into 'unknowing' by way of participation.

James Alison provides a striking account of the theologian's vocation that captures much of what I am suggesting:

> The theologian's vocation requires participating on the inside of an act of communication coming from someone who is not an object in the universe. And the notion of the Creator, far from being bad science concerning the beginning of the universe, involves us in undergoing a sense of 'something coming out of nothing'.[17]

To say that creation comes 'from nothing' is not so much a statement about an independent state of affairs, as though it were a hypothesis about the first instant of the universe, but an invitation to 'undergo' divine things. It is a way of acknowledging our dependence on a free Creator who gives all things 'to be'; but more, it is a summons to live out that dependency, wakefully and through the responsible exercise of our freedom, in such a way that we *continue* to undergo God's self-communicating act of creation. This is hardly the special reserve of those who call themselves 'theologians', of course, but Alison reminds us that the work of theology, even in its disciplined and professional aspects, is a vocation that summons those who approach it as a way of life. With reference to Thomas Aquinas, and Dionysius the Areopagite before him, Alison's account of theology as a certain *pati divina* implies far more than the production of ideas that bear upon what we call 'God', 'Christ', or 'salvation'. It implies a process of change, of being 'on the way', so to speak, in which the theologian participates, actively, but with a disposition of deepest welcoming, in a divine happening that is ongoing. It entails an 'attitudinal pattern, lived over time' that avails oneself 'to a stretched and stressed openness to "something from nothing" …'.[18]

It is precisely here where contemplative practice becomes crucial for the work of theology. There are many reasons why this is so, but at least one reason immediately stands out: contemplation is not a discursive strategy that tries to formulate in words, in turns of phrase, in paradoxes, in clashing metaphors, in narrative subversions, or in argument the ungraspable mystery of God. It may accompany all of this, and no doubt is prepared by it.[19] And yet the practice of contemplation – and here I am referring specifically to non-discursive meditation and prayer – seeks to inhabit that mystery through a long 'letting go'. Contemplative prayer unsettles our managed impressions and conceptual maps and invites us to discover a more fundamental awareness that cannot be exhausted by any of its contents. It is rather like 'free-falling' into an abyss, as Coakley suggestively puts it, but in this case we will find ourselves graciously upheld by an ineffable presence that is always there, as close as closeness itself, but which is usually not noticed by us on account of our many preoccupations, mental chatter, and restless search for identity. In this 'formless' mode of prayer, which is by no means opposed to discursive approaches of prayer, we release our thoughts and concepts about God in the obscurity of faith, even those that are most ennobling and consoling, and settle into an attentive repose, a deep stillness that allows us to become wakeful to the mystery of God in our midst, just as it is. 'Preserve a loving attentiveness to God with no desire to feel or understand any particular thing concerning him', writes Saint John of the Cross, in simple summary of a practice that, when cultivated over time, is transformative.[20]

It should be observed that while various traditions of contemplative prayer may recommend certain body postures, watchfulness of breath, or rhythmic recitations of a prayer word or short phrase in order to centre one's attention – and to this extent there is a certain skilfulness and habit-formation involved – by no means should such practices be regarded as the deployment of techniques in order to acquire special states of mind or generate heightened experiences. Contemplative practice 'doesn't acquire anything', writes Martin Laird. 'In that sense, and an important sense, it is not a technique but a surrendering of deeply imbedded resistances that allows the sacred within gradually to reveal itself as a simple, fundamental fact'.[21] Laird adds that this is not a 'search for God-as-object-to-be-acquired', but the release of our tenacious grip on things in order that we may grow wakeful to God's presence with simplicity of attention.[22] We enter into this loving attentiveness by releasing our affective defences and by unclasping our cognitive designs, by unsettling and letting go of the steady stream of sensations, thoughts, and entangled desires that ordinarily structure our awareness, and which often project the illusion that we are separated from God. Whereas we often imagine God as a reality 'out there', or perhaps an 'absence' that requires some method of recovery, contemplative practice relinquishes our tendency to formulate God's 'otherness' in a quasi-objective way and slowly awakens us to the self-communicating mystery of God that animates our very existence.

> God is the ground of the human being ... [and so] if we are going to speak of what a human being is, we have not said enough until we speak of God. If we are to discover for ourselves who we truly are – that inmost self that is known before it is formed, ever hidden with Christ in God (Ps 139:13; Jer. 1:5; Col. 3:3) – the discovery is going to be a manifestation of the ineffable mystery of God, though we may feel more and more inclined to say less and less about God.[23]

Discovering God in this way, through the embodied practice of unknowing, may seem like the negation of our agency or the absorption of our identity, but this is a mistaken notion. Our dependence upon God is not at all opposed to our creaturely freedom, for we wouldn't even be creaturely were it not for God who ceaselessly gives us 'to be'. In point of fact, we should say the exact opposite: the more we live into the freedom and vitality of the Creator who summons forth all things, the more we participate in God's own freedom and vitality in the realization of our own creatureliness. Our inviolable dignity is discovered *in* God, not in a separative, agonistic movement away from God. 'Some call this differentiating union', Laird notes: 'the more we realize are one with God the more we become ourselves, just as we are, just as we were created to be. The Creator is outpouring love, the creation, the love outpoured'.[24] A better formulation of 'the distinction' would be hard to find.

Contemplative prayer helps us gain a lived sense that God is not a 'Big Other' against whom we must strive in the search for identity. Because God is not 'over against' anything at all, or in competition with any creature, this means that our relationship with God is the one relationship that allows us fully to accept our creatureliness, our contingency and finitude, without any fear or resentment whatsoever, without any need to buffer ourselves in the attempt to secure identity against non-being. With God, and God alone, we may say 'yes' to our deepest vulnerability as pure gift. Rowan Williams makes this point beautifully, and with explicit reference to *creatio ex nihilo*:

> To say, 'I exist (along with the whole of my environment) at God's will, I am unconditionally dependent upon God' means [that] ... my existence in the world, *including* my need to imagine this as personal, active and giving, is 'of God'; my search for an identity is something rooted in God's freedom, which grounds the sheer thereness of the shared world I stand in ... Before the literally inconceivable fact of the divine difference and the divine liberty we have no words except thanksgiving that, because God's life *is what it is*, we are ... The contemplation of God, which is among other things the struggle to become the kind of person who can without fear be open to the divine activity, would not be possible if God were seen as an agent exercising power over others, bending them to the divine will.

Contemplative prayer classically finds its focus in the awareness of God at the centre of the praying person's being – and, simultaneously, God at the centre of the whole world's being: a solidarity in creatureliness.[25]

4.   Love without a why

There are two features of this quotation that I would like to highlight by way of conclusion. The first is that its appeal to contemplative prayer provides an indispensable resource for gaining a lived sense of *creatio ex nihilo* – from the inside, as it were. By relaxing into our creatureliness through the surrendering of the deeply embedded resistances we have towards it, we do not negate our creaturely identities or capacities for action but in fact allow them to grow open to the ineffable source and ground of our creatureliness, to the creator God who gives us the gift of being and who allows us to respond to that gift in freedom and love. Our creatureliness is 'from nothing', which is to say, 'wholly from God', and this implies no contradiction with our dignity as creatures. We are really and truly 'other' than God, and our distinction from God is a gift, not an ontological rupture from an original, absorbing unity we must strive to recover. And yet, our 'otherness' is not a barrier to God's unconditioned presence. God may infinitely transcend all created reality, but this transcendence is the most immanent reality of our lives, which means that God and creation are 'not two'. Contemplative practice is critically important to help us gain an enhanced sense of this inexhaustible fact, not least because it entails our letting go of various ways we might regard God as a kind of object. It is a *non-dual awareness* that is the hallmark of contemplative practice, and its cultivation is a way of knowing by unknowing.

The second feature of Williams's quote worth highlighting is the sheer wonderment that comes when we recognize that creation does not have to be – and yet it is. *Creatio ex nihilo* is really a contemplative insight. It is an invitation to discover our creaturely contingency as an inexhaustible gift, a gift that is more original than any violence, destruction, or despair that might be befall us. And notice how it issues this invitation: through a breathtaking denial. Perhaps we are not accustomed to thinking of the theology of creation as a work of apophasis, i.e., as a way of 'unsaying' or 'unknowing', but we should. In fact, the theology of creation from nothing is as thoroughgoing a denial as one can find in Christian theology. For although it does indeed *affirm* that creation is a gift from God – an expression of God's boundless freedom and love, an 'overflowing' of God's triune life, etc. – it *denies* that creation is finally a matter of comprehension. We cannot lay claim to the depths of our own creatureliness, for they spring from God's own unfathomable freedom. The creature does not stand out from itself alone, or even the sum of creaturely relations, for creatureliness itself does not have to be. In this sense, creation is 'without a why', as Meister Eckhart was fond of saying. There is no 'reason' why it must be. No logical or metaphysical necessity undergirds it. Though we may come to learn a great deal about the processes and nexus of relations that contribute to its history of becoming, the very fact that anything exists at all, rather than nothing, is not amenable to comprehension, even as it evokes our endless astonishment.

And we should add that this 'without a why' is very different from any nihilistic interpretation that regards the non-necessity of creation as absurd. On the contrary, it points to the sheer delight in there being anything at all. It is primordially *good* to be, and this goodness has to do with the Creator who freely wishes to impart the goodness of being to others – for their own sake. Creation is love outpoured, to recall Laird's phrase, and such love is unconditional, or agapeic, because it is given without compulsion, without reserve, without ulterior motive, and without any need to regard what it loves as a rival. It is wholly *for* the other, and in this sense, it loves 'from nothing'.

Notes

1 Sarah Coakley, *God, Sexuality, and the Self: An Essay 'On the Trinity'* (Cambridge: Cambridge University Press, 2013), p. 41.
2 Ibid., p. 41.
3 See Part One of Sarah Coakley, *Submissions and Powers: Spirituality, Philosophy, and Gender* (Oxford: Blackwell Publishers, 2002).
4 Coakley, *God, Sexuality, and the Self*, pp. 45–6.
5 Ibid., p. 43.
6 Peter Harrison masterfully traces the shifting senses of theology as a 'scientific' enterprise in his recently published Gifford Lectures, showing that throughout antiquity and much of the medieval period it explicitly meant an ascetical and contemplative 'way of life' that entailed a host of embodied virtues and mental habits, rather than an independent body of knowledge. See his *The Territories of Science and Religion* (Chicago: University of Chicago Press, 2015).
7 See Pierre Hadot, *Philosophy as a Way of Life*, trans. Arnold I. Davidson (Oxford: Blackwell, 1995). See also his *What is Ancient Philosophy?*, trans. Michael Chase (Cambridge, MA: Harvard University Press, 2002).
8 Ibid., 46.
9 For two examples of such critiques, see Catherine Keller, *The Face of the Deep: A Theology of Becoming* (London: Routledge, 2003) and John D. Caputo, *The Weakness of God: A Theology of the Event* (Bloomington, IN: Indiana University Press, 2005).
10 Gerhard May, *Creatio ex nihilo: The Doctrine of 'Creation out of Nothing' in Early Christian Thought* (Edinburgh: T&T Clark, 1994), p. 176.
11 For an incisive account of 'the distinction', see Robert Sokolowski, *The God of Faith and Reason: Foundations of Christian Theology* (Notre Dame: University of Notre Dame Press, 1982). See also Kathryn Tanner's 'non-competitive' account of the God-world relation in her *God and Creation in Christian Theology: Tyranny or Empowerment?* (Minneapolis: Fortress Press, 1988).
12 David Bentley Hart, *The Experience of God: Being, Consciousness, Bliss* (New Haven, CT: Yale University Press, 2013), p. 107.
13 Karl Rahner, *Foundations of Christian Faith: An Introduction to the Idea of Christianity*, trans. William V. Dych (New York: Crossroad, 1978), p. 62. My italics.
14 Thomas Halík, *Patience with God: The Story of Zacchaeus Continuing in Us*, trans. Gerald Turner (New York: Doubleday, 2009), p. 121.
15 David B. Burrell, *Knowing the Unknowable God: Ibn-Sina, Maimonides, Aquinas* (Notre Dame, IN: University of Notre Dame Press, 1992), p. 17.
16 Herbert McCabe, *God Matters* (London: Continuum, 1987), p. 7.

17 James Alison, *Undergoing God: Dispatches From the Scene of a Break-In* (New York: Continuum, 2006), p. 4.

18 Ibid., p. 5.

19 As Denys Turner reminds us, it is a mistake to oppose contemplative silence and speech about God, just as it is false to oppose apophasis and cataphasis in general. With reference to the Pseudo-Dionysian corpus and its enormous influence in the history of Christian theology, he notes that all apophasis 'presupposes the cataphatic "dialectically" in the sense that the silence of the negative way is the silence achieved only at the point at which talk about God has been exhausted' ('Apophaticism, Idolatry, and the Claims of Reason', in *Silence and the Word: Negative Theology and Incarnation*, ed. Oliver Davies and Denys Turner (Cambridge: Cambridge University Press, 2002), p. 18.

20 Saint John of the Cross, 'Sayings of Light and Love', in *The Collected Works of St. John of the Cross*, trans. Kevin Kavanaugh, O.C.D. and Otilio Rodriguez, O.C.D (Washington, DC: ICS Publications, rev. ed. 1991), §88, p. 91.

21 Martin Laird, O.S.A., *Into the Silent Land: A Guide to the Christian Practice of Contemplation* (Oxford: Oxford University Press, 2006), p. 8.

22 Ibid., p. 80.

23 Ibid., p. 9.

24 Ibid., p. 17.

25 Rowan Williams, *On Christian Theology* (Oxford: Blackwell Publishers, 2000), pp. 74, 75–6.

3 The Trinity as our ascetic programme

Nikolaï Sakharov

This chapter presents the spirituality of the Orthodox monastic tradition as it is practised in the monastic community of St John the Baptist in Essex. Any visitor who enters the refectory of the Monastery will, without fail, notice a large mural painting representing the Holy Trinity, which is based on the celebrated Rublev's icon of the three angels at Abraham's table. The fresco was painted by the founder of the monastery – Fr Sophrony Sakharov. He spent over 20 years as a monk on Mt Athos in Greece and then moved to Europe and finally to the UK, where he established the monastery in 1959, and then spiritually nourished the community until his death in 1993. In this painting there is a remarkable detail: the inscription that quotes the Book of Genesis (1:26): 'Let us create man in our own image and after our likeness'.

For monastic spirituality within the Orthodox tradition, this vision of humanity created in the image of the Holy Trinity is something that has not always been expressed so explicitly. In Christendom as a whole, and in Protestantism particularly, there has been a trend aptly summarized by Robin Parry:

> For many Christians the Trinity has become something akin to an appendix: it is there, but they're not sure what its function is, they get by in life without it doing very much, and if they had to have it removed they wouldn't be too distressed.[1]

Or, as Peter Toon says: 'there is a general feeling that the Trinity is both difficult and unimportant'.[2]

However, in Christianity there has been a welcome development made within the past sixty years: we may call it a renaissance of trinitarian thought in the academic world. In Western Christianity, a valuable impetus comes earlier from Karl Barth (1932), who reemphasized the importance of dogma in general and of the doctrine of the Trinity in particular. In the UK, as we know, in the late 1970s there were some valuable ecumenical contributions made in a series of books under the title *The Forgotten Trinity*.

The founder of the Monastery of St John the Baptist (in Essex) – Fr Sophrony – was very much aware of these developments, as his own theological vision can be defined as 'trinitarian', in the sense that the doctrine of the Trinity was at the heart of his theology and anthropology.

One may see this interest in, and focus on, the Trinity as a historical and intellectual legacy of his Russian background. Fedor Dostoyevsky (1821–1881), with his usual idealistic aspiration, believed that the Russians are called to reach 'universality', to become 'pan-human', that 'the Russian heart longs for the panhuman brotherhood of men'. However, in reality the Russians have long displayed a chronic inability to live in unity: so as to embrace ideological and political differences. From medieval times, the segmented princedoms on the Russian land wasted their existence in fighting each other, thereby becoming easy prey to Tartar-Mongol invaders.

This land craved some sort of a uniting principle – as a matter of survival. And, in the fourteenth century, a Russian monk named Sergius of Radonezh appealed to his brethren, and through them in turn to the whole land of Russia, to become one – united – as the Trinity is One: to that end, he built a chapel and dedicated it to the Name of the Holy Trinity. For theologically poor Russia, it was a message of unprecedented theological boldness, which made him a father of the Russian nation. His call for unity in the image of the Trinity united the Russian forces into a state, feeble though it was, but yet the one that secured their victory over the Tartar-Mongol invaders. Not long after St. Sergius, Andrey Rublev painted his famous icon of the Trinity (ca. 1411). This icon has since been the silent, yet ever-present, guardian of St. Sergius' remarkable message, which waited to be rediscovered later. As a visible image, the icon silently formed the hearts and minds of the Russian people.

In the nineteenth century Russian thinkers rediscovered the bounty of the hidden theological, ideological, political treasures of the doctrine of Trinity. The principle of Triunity became a rich source of inspiration for various aspects of human culture and for the life of Russian society. Here I want to mention Nikolai Fedorov (1829–1903), whose celebrated formula I have borrowed for the title of this chapter by replacing the word social with the word ascetic. He writes: 'The Trinity is our social project'.

Russian literature of the nineteenth century was marked by an underlying awareness that the realization of one's human potential and of one's personhood are impossible in a vacuum, in the absence of other people: the human person can realize itself only in relation to, and in communion with, other people through humbly erasing the dividing boundaries erected by egoism.[3] This perception of personhood, as *Amo ergo sum*, defines the literary and poetic climate of nineteenth-century Russia, before it was rediscovered by theologians. The words of a leading intellectual figure of nineteenth-century Russia, Bissarion G. Belinsky (1811–1848), aptly reflect the prevailing fashion: 'Do not forget, oh man, that your infinite and ultimate bliss consists in melting your ego in love: renounce yourself, live for the happiness of others, sacrifice everything for the happiness of others.'[4] The beauty of this ideal shines in the poetry, for example, in Eugeny Baratynsky (1800–1844) and in many literary works such as Dostoyevsky's *The Idiot* (1869), with its main character, Prince Myshkin,[5] and in *The Brothers Karamazov* (1880), or in Leo Tolstoy's *Resurrection* (1899) where Tolstoy places great emphasis on his message 'to serve others before self'. At the same time, Russian literature shamed egoism and the inability to open up to others in love as a true sign of illness of the soul, to the degradation and disintegration of human person. This was well portrayed in Dostoyevsky's *Crime and Punishment* (1866) or in Nikolai Gogol's comic characters.[6]

In religious thought the Russians rediscovered the Trinity theologically: as the model, as the universal principle of unity.[7] Thus, Vladimir Soloviev focuses on the concept of 'pan-unity',[8] while others worked out the ideals of relationship that can secure this unity, starting long before Soloviev with Alexey Khomyakov and his concept of *conciliarity*.[9] By the twentieth century Russian religious thought finally crystallized this general sense that the image and likeness of God in man is not an individual category – the image is a dynamic inter-relationship within the whole of mankind, a multiplicity of persons living in unity, the communion of persons. The Trinity is a supreme example of how people can live together in perfect communion. The connecting string for the oneness of humanity becomes the objective of Russian religious thought. 'The Russians wanted to bring to the world the ideal of pan-unity', Thomas Špidlík observes, so the Tri-Unity is seen by Russians as their vocation.[10]

Later, in the twentieth century, when this image of the Trinity was refracted through a prism of genius of such theological giants as Fr Sergius Bulgakov and Fr Paul Florensky, trinitarian thought was taken to a new level altogether. They both discovered that the distance between the Prototype – God and His image – and humanity is not so remote as a mere analogy. There is a correlation and kinship, which in itself is 'a profound pastoral and soteriological message', as Meerson evaluates in Bulgakov's theological legacy.[11]

Speaking of 'a conformity or *co-imagedness* between Divinity and humanity', Bulgakov asserts: 'The humanity of Divinity and the divinity of humanity are given pre-eternally in God.'[12] The very idea of 'image' presupposes not unilateral but bilateral affinity. Not only is humanity a reflection of God, but also God is a reflection of humanity: humanity in some way is already eternally contained within the Godhead. In God everything is human-like. 'If the human being has the image of God, this means that in some sense beyond precise explanation God has the image of the human being. Just as man carries the image of God, God also has man's image.'[13]

Sergius Bulgakov always admired St. Sergius of Radonezh for the legacy of his act when he named the chapel in his monastery after the Holy Trinity: this fact inspired Bulgakov to see in the Trinity the ultimate example of *perichoretic kenotic love*.[14] He comments, with great enthusiasm, that: 'Love is seen as the very life of the divine unity of the Three ... It is the eternal act of love-in-mutuality, where Three are One and One are Three. And Man is created after the image of this God'.[15] Bulgakov believes that every human *person* is trinitarian, as it were, in their very constitution: 'Thou' is another 'I', and at the same time a similar 'I', which is also 'Not-I', because it is beyond 'I', but it is given to me as the condition of my self-consciousness, thus it is in me. 'I' cannot remain in its self-enclosedness, in its metaphysical egoism, but it has need of 'Thou' to become 'I', in order to realize the fullness of its self-being.

On this basis Bulgakov arrives at the concept of the 'undividedness of mutual reflection'. Yet he speaks of the insufficiency of bi-unity, and warns against the possibility of 'Thou' turning into a mere 'version' of 'I'. For the affirmation and recognition of 'I' in 'Thou', there is a need for the third person. As an expression of 'I' in other *personae* Bulgakov uses 'We', which is the self-realization of 'I' in multi-unity. From his principle Bulgakov deduces the catholicity (*sobornost*) of any personal being: *Sobornost* (catholicity), or multi-unity, is an inherent attribute of the personal 'I' – hypostasis, without which 'I' cannot realize itself or even exist: saying 'I', hypostasis at the same time says also 'Thou', 'We', 'They'.[16] To summarize, Bulgakov writes:

> The fullness of the image of God in man, rooted in persona, goes beyond persona as a monad, into the multi-unity of all mankind. One may say, that the image of God in its fullness belongs not even to man in his one persona, but to humankind in its *sobornost*, in love after the image of the consubstantial triunity of God.[17]

Thomas Špidlík calls Paul Florensky 'the theologian par excellence of the Trinity'.[18] Indeed, Florensky sees the Trinity doctrine as the key that unlocks the mysteries of the whole of creation.[19] For him, the trinitarian principles manifest themselves everywhere: in the universe, in society, in philosophical thinking, in human relationships.

The word 'consubstantial' becomes very important: the Church is not a mere get-together, a 'synagogue'. The members of the Church do not gather together, they *are* really united into one, their unity is *consubstantial as in the Trinity*.[20] This was a very helpful safeguard of authentic depth in understanding human interrelationship. The participants in the Eucharist are invited to glorify the name of the Trinity with one mouth and one heart. Florensky emphasizes that we say with one heart (*homoousios*) and not with a similarity of hearts (*homoiousios*). Our unity and our love are not just moral ethics; they are *ontological* categories.[21]

What Russian religious thought had achieved *in theory*, Fr Sophrony applied *in practice* to monastic community life. He writes:

> The monastic community sets out to achieve unity … in the image of the oneness of the Holy Trinity … each one of us in some sense within his own hypostasis, is the centre of all … There is no one greater, no one lesser.[22]

The Trinity thereby becomes our ascetic project; the prime target of all our ascetic endeavours is to achieve love for others like the love we see in the Divine Prototype – the Trinity. When an Orthodox monastery was set up in a remote village in Essex in 1959, local residents, who did not know much about Orthodox monasticism, were rather concerned about such an unusual presence: they saw bearded long-haired people wearing black cassocks. One of the locals asked his bishop: 'Who are these people? Are they a kind of a sect? Do they believe in the Holy Trinity?' The local bishop reassured him: 'Don't worry – they are Orthodox, they are the ones who invented the Trinity in the first place'.

To this comment Orthodox ascetics would probably add that their aim is to *practise* the Trinity.

Orthodox asceticism favours, *de facto*, the practical implications of Christian dogma, and organically shuns what might be called 'abstract theology'. If theology doesn't relate to daily life in a concrete practical sense, it resides outside the scope of interests of an Orthodox ascetic. This attitude to theology in modern Orthodox monasticism has been dogmatically articulated in Russian religious thought. By breaking through the confines of the sheer rationality of Aristotelian logic, it promoted what might be called 'existential theology', by acknowledging the limits of human rational thinking in dealing with Divine revelation, which exceeds human intellectual resources, proposing instead a holistic approach to its appropriation that would incorporate the totality of human being, focusing on the heart as the uniting spiritual principle in man's constitution: 'If our intellect detaches itself from the heart and from faith, and undertakes to approach the Revelation with its own laws of reasoning, the Revelation would present insoluble problems.'[23] Thus, Frs Sergius Bulgakov and Paul Florensky did away with what might be called a conceptual algebra. Instead, Fr Paul Florensky establishes antinomy as the most authentic method in dealing with theological categories.[24] The distinctive idea of knowledge in general, and of theology in particular, implied first and foremost for these thinkers: *communion and participation* in the object of knowledge.[25]

For an Orthodox ascetic knowledge is understood as 'a fusion' in very being,[26] 'communion of being'.[27] Theological knowledge in monasticism is associated, above all, with the actual experience of personal communion with Divine reality through unceasing prayer and contemplation, which constitutes the prime reality for the monk. Theology, thereby, becomes an existential *Gestalt*. Church dogmas and theology form and define the content of ascetic life: they become a *typicon*; that is, the rule and basis of daily monastic discipline. An Orthodox spirituality naturally shuns 'non-dogmatic faith, non-ecclesiological Christianity and non-ascetic Christianity'. For the monk 'the Church, dogma and asceticism – constitute one single life'.[28] Monasticism stimulates in ascetics a very fine sensitivity to any dogmatic detail, since each aspect of dogma finds its reflection in daily life and spirituality. Hence, any deviation from the dogmatic vision would inevitably result in major changes to religious practices. The dogma of the Trinity and its interpretation were of prime significance for Orthodox ascetics:

> The life of each and every Christian confession is conditioned at all levels by its conception of the Holy Trinity. Differences in theological interpretation of the principle of the Person – Hypostasis in the Divine Being

constitute a watershed, a demarcation line, not only between the various religions but between the sundry Christian confessions too.[29]

Such a 'detailed' dogmatic vision of ascetic practices impels one to look beyond external aspects of monastic vows and to go deeper to the very basis of monastic life, to the very heart of human existence, so as to live in accordance with the Divine revelation that mankind is a replica of God the Trinity and the heir of the life of the Trinity. Russian religious thought had provided a solid theoretical foundation to delve into the understanding of the interpersonal relationship of the Personae within the Trinity. Notably, Fr Sergius Bulgakov, in his renowned trilogy *O Bogochelovechestve* (1933, 1936 and 1945), with an unprecedented extensiveness, spells out the principles of relationship within the Trinity, as they are presented in the Johannine gospel particularly.[30] This theology is taken up as a guideline for monastic community. Even though the Johannine references to the inner interpersonal life of the Trinity[31] are not set out like Christ's commandments, they do become so if the Trinity is seen as a model and prototype. These references provide an image of authentic relationship, which lead to a oneness of being that is featured in the Johannine prayer of Christ (Jn 17:11). This oneness, therefore, is seen by the evangelist John as the final testament of God to humankind and the ultimate revelation about humanity that inherits from the Godhead oneness of the three *personae*.

Monasticism focuses on the fact that there is no closer reality in our lives than our relationships with other people; thus, there is no other idea or dogma more relevant to our daily life than the prototype of the Trinity. Relationship is the divine legacy to God's image: we are able to love like God, to imitate the relationship of the Divine personae: 'The persona does not determine himself by opposition. His is an attitude of love. Love is the most profound content of his being, the noblest expression of his essence. In this love lies the likeness to God, Who is Love.'[32]

In the Orthodox Church there is the obvious prevalence of coenobitic monasticism over the heremitic life-style; much of its spiritual teaching focuses upon the monk's relationship with his fellow brothers. Athonite spirituality is particularly sensitive to the communal aspect of monastic rules, aptly summarized by an Athonite saint: 'Our brother is our life.'[33] This spirituality proceeds from a profound awareness of the trinitarian paradigm that shapes the ultimate aim of monastic strivings – to attain authentic God-like integrity of relationship with other personae. The framework of Orthodox asceticism differs from henotheistic ascetic traditions (Judaism, Islam) as well as from polytheistic religions, in which the paradigm of communal existence is not as articulately defined as it is in Christian monotheism.

Relationship emerges as the cornerstone of ascetic spirituality – *amo ergo sum*: *alterum* (that is any other person) becomes the content of *ego*: '*Thou* art my life'. According to the Athonite monastic tradition the presence (or absence) of Divine grace is manifested above all in terms of the relationship and attitude towards others. An Athonite ascetic writes: 'Grace proceeds from brotherly love, and by brotherly love is grace preserved.'[34] 'Monasticism is a form of love.'[35] And there are endless ways in which we can express and realize trinitarian life, how to forget oneself for the sake of another persona.

The more the monk shifts his existential concerns from *ego* towards *alii* (others) the larger is the scope of his love. The final aim of the monastic life is realized when a monk reaches the universal scale and prays for the whole world and embraces the unity of the whole human race as one being. In this spiritual state of prayer for the whole world, the Divine image of tri-unity finds its actual perfect realization. The human person is called upon 'to achieve the fullness of god-manhood', 'to become dynamically equal to humanity in the aggregate' just as the divine hypostasis is to the Trinity.[36] 'Man as hypostasis is a principle uniting the plurality of cosmic being; capable of containing the fullness of divine and human life.'[37]

In modern biblical scholarship only very few commentators see the correspondence between the idea of unity and oneness in John 17:11 and the 'trinitarian' reading of Genesis 1:26.[38] This Johannine passage can be seen as an indication of the purpose of the entire *Heilsgeschichte*, i.e., the Divine economy of salvation of the human race. The fourth Gospel thus presents the work of Christ as the restoration of the primeval unity of human fellowship in the trinitarian image. The history of God's salvific covenants displays a certain tendency to broaden the scope of unity. After the 'fall' of Adam (Gen. 3:6–7), the fratricidal story of Cain and Abel (Gen. 4:8) portrays the deranged aftermath of the fall as the disintegration[39] and atomization of human relationships.[40] The first covenant with Noah (Gen. 6:18) marks the restoration of unity within the primitive unit of human *commune* – the family. The later covenants with Abraham (Gen. 22:17) and Moses (Gen. 34:27) point to the achievement of unity on a larger scale: the nation. The ultimate goal is the universal embrace of the whole of humanity. This is the crowning work of Christ and the Holy Spirit that 'called all men to unity', according to the Orthodox hymn of Pentecost. Every Orthodox coenobitic monastery is, therefore, understood to be a microcosm of the restored unity of the whole of humanity, where all nations learn to live in unity after the image and likeness of the Holy Trinity with the ultimate purpose of achieving this all-embracing love. As Archimandrite Sophrony writes: 'If in our monastic life we do not learn to love, then I don't find any justification for monasticism as a way of life.'[41]

Monks in the Orthodox Church are traditionally expected to give four promises or vows: to abide 1) in poverty, 2) in chastity, 3) in obedience, 4) and in the monastery where the vows are given. These monastic vows within the Orthodox perspective are considered to be a reflection of the trinitarian image. The monastic practice of *poverty*, non-acquisition, is often seen as a life of self-deprivation. Yet for an Orthodox ascetic it has a different meaning. The vow of poverty does not imply that one shuns possessions as something intrinsically evil. Poverty is understood to be an eternal act of *sharing with others* – a trinitarian act. It is the image of trinitarian love that becomes the inner imperative to share one's substance with his consubstantial fellow human. Thus, poverty is not so much a state, but is an act of dynamic manifestation of real ontological communion in being. This understanding of poverty is rooted in the ethics of wealth that are set out in Luke's writing.[42] In the parable of the Rich Man and Lazarus (Luke 16:19–31), the rich man is denied a human name, and thereby the status of a human person, not because of his wealth but because of his lack of love and non-sharing with the poverty-stricken Lazarus. As Denise Tucker points out: 'Abraham reminds the rich man of his lack of compassion during his lifetime towards Lazarus',[43] failing to realize the image of God and remaining self-enclosed in his egoism: it is the latter who constitutes an unbridgeable chasm between the fellowship of persons and separated individual, incapable of communion with others. Zaccheus (Luke 19:2–10), on the contrary, finds his human integrity, understood as 'salvation' (Luke 19:9) through the loving act of 'sharing fellowship',[44] and not in the mere disposing of possessions (Luke 19:8). Therefore, monastic poverty is rooted in the principles of fellowship set out in Acts (2:44–45). The founder of the Orthodox community in Essex writes: 'all that the monk has and his whole self, he surrenders to each and all.'[45]

The same can be said about the vow of chastity. The Greek word for chastity, *sophrosyne*, conveys the literal meaning as 'wholeness', 'integrity of one's being'. Chastity in the trinitarian context goes far beyond a mere abstinence from sexual contact and becomes an expression of love in the trinitarian mode of being that excludes *de facto* any shift of existential concern from 'the beloved' to anything that is 'not the beloved'. It is rooted in the Christological concept of 'faithfulness of Christ' (Phil. 3:9), as 'the exemplar of the type of faithfulness that a believer is to reproduce in his or her own life'.[46] This understanding of the vow of chastity is supported by the vow of living in the same monastery. Achieving love for all the brethren excludes any possibility of changing the monastery because of failure in establishing an authentic trinitarian relationship with the brethren, irrespective of their behaviour. Departure from the community is seen as an act of breaking the unity, contrary to the unifying work of Christ to achieve the oneness of humanity (cf. Jn 17:11). Orthodox asceticism makes a significant contribution to the understanding of monastic *obedience* by setting this practice within the context of trinitarian theology.

Orthodox monastic obedience is not a compliance or discipline based on a set of rules. It is a *personal* act of love and expression of *personal* love. Love implies an appropriation of the beloved's will, the fulfilment of which becomes an existential drive for the person who loves, to the extent that the beloved becomes the rule of one's existence. There is an underlying idea of this in the gospel of John 'the Word becoming flesh' (John 1:14), when a commandment becomes a person. This is very much reflected in the Johannine concept of the *hypodeigma* (example) of Christ (Jn 13:15), whose own personality is manifested in actions, as a commandment for believers to follow.

Orthodox Athonite spirituality asserts that anything that is imposed upon a free person, or compromises his freedom of will has no lasting spiritual value.[47] Spiritual progress in the ascetic virtue of love cannot be ensured by a set of rules, discipline or external authority (if *authority* is understood as lordship). The

Synoptic Gospels reject such a vision of authority as intrinsically *pagan* in Mt 20:25–26.[48] The latter passage highlights an inherent antithesis between love, as fulfilling the will of others, and authority, as imposition of one's own will on others. The essence of Christian personhood, as it is professed by Eastern Orthodox monastic ethics, consists in focusing on concerns for others, so that the others become the content of one's life, and on the opposite end, Luciferism implies that one implements one's own *ego* as the content of life for others.

Eastern monastic spirituality dwells on the Johannine understanding of the concept of *exousia*, which thrusts its meaning forth as *capacity*: 'exousia (authority) to become the children of God' (Jn 1:12).[49] There is a distinctive understanding of *exousia* within the monastic community and within the Orthodox Church as a whole. It acknowledges

> the fact of inequality, hierarchy, division into upper and lower, into overlord and servant; but Christ turns the pyramid upside down. The incontestable apex of this pyramid is the Son of man, and He says of Himself that He came not to be ministered unto but to minister, and to give his life a ransom for many (Matt. 20:28) and whosoever will be chief among you, let him be your servant (Matt. 20:27). Here we are shown both the designation and the *raison d'être* of the ecclesiastical hierarchy – to raise those low in the spiritual scale to a higher degree of perfection. Christ took upon Himself the burden of the sin of the whole world. He is the summit of the inverted pyramid, the summit on which the whole weight of the pyramid of being depends. In an inexplicable way those who follow after Christ become like Him, taking upon themselves the burden of others' infirmities.[50]

Thus, *exousia*, in the context of ecclesiastical and monastic authority, is understood after the image of the supreme authority of Christ (see Matt. 28:18) as the capacity of carrying the weight and the burden of all the brothers and sisters. 'The Christian goes downwards, into the depths of the overturned pyramid where the crushing weight is concentrated – to the place where the Lord is, who took upon Himself the sins of the whole world – Christ'.[51] An Orthodox ascetic is expected to imitate the consistent pattern of behaviour displayed by Christ as He is presented by all four evangelists, which avoids any striving towards secular authority, as it is affirmed from the outset of the Gospel narrative in the *pericope* of Christ's temptation (Luke 4:7).

This Orthodox ascetic perception of 'lordship' – authority as the consistent existential *Gestalt* portrayed by the evangelists in the paradigm of Christ – finds its further manifestation in the complexity of Christ's interpersonal communication, and thereby provides an interesting answer as to why the historical Jesus employed parables. Entering the arena of modern biblical scholarship, Orthodox monasticism, on the basis of its practical experience,[52] suggests that *parables* are a unique form of personal communication (different from impersonal information): while being addressed personally, a parable leaves the freedom of its hearers intact by veiling the ego of the author-speaker,[53] thus avoiding any forceful imposition of the speaker's ego upon hearers.[54] This understanding of the parabolic language is well summarized by W. H. Auden: 'You cannot tell people what to do, you can tell them a parable.'[55]

For a Christian ascetic, the parabolic paradigm of interpersonal communication ensures that obedience is exercised not out of necessity or as subjection to a stronger power or authority, but out of the personal love that *naturally* moves the ascetic to do the will of the beloved. This theology, once again, derives from the trinitarian perception of authority and obedience: when the beloved person becomes your rule, commandment and living principle. This mode of being is illustrated by the patristic trinitarian concept of *perichoresis* (inter-coinherence)[56]: it is a dynamic movement of love, of desire to do the other person's will, the everlasting and dynamic exchange of giving space to each other. The patristic idea of the *monarchy* of the Father,[57] as the Prime Mover, consists in initiating this movement of love within the Trinity: in the pre-eternal act of generation of the Son and emanation of the Holy Spirit the Father conveys His fullness (τὰ πάντα) unto the Son (Matt. 11:27), which is further passed to His alter-ego, the *Paraclete* (John 14:16). Walter Kasper summarizes the monarchy of the Father in a remarkable formula of 'the groundless ground of a self-communicating love'[58] who 'eternally and without beginning brings forth the Son and the Holy Spirit and unites with them in the *perichoresis* of love'.[59] Monastic humility imitates this *perichoresis*: 'Love transfers the existence of the person who loves into the beloved, thus the person assimilates the life of the beloved',[60] and 'the existence of the beloved people whom I love becomes the content of my life … If I, like Christ, love all to the end (Jn 13:1), then the being of all becomes my own being through the power of love.'[61]

Within such a trinitarian perspective monastic obedience excludes anything that is non-personal or supra-personal. Love, as a personal category, cannot be exercised within the realm of the impersonal: one cannot love the rule, one can only love a person. Within Orthodox spirituality, the obedience is exclusively an interpersonal discipline: monks obey (i.e. listen to and hear) a person (*staretz*), not the rule. That is why Orthodox monasticism shuns any institutional 'orders' as they are found in other ascetic traditions. When I was still a student at university a friend of mine asked me: 'So you are a monk. To which order do you belong?' I replied: 'In the Orthodox Church we don't have orders, we have *disorder*, and I follow this disorder, I guess'. This disorder, can be understood to express the prevalence of personal principle in monastic asceticism, in which each person is given a wide scope for personal development, avoiding thereby any pre-set path:

> The principle of personalistic obedience – derives from our theological concept of … the Holy Trinity.…The loss of, or deviation from, this theology would lead to the conscious or unconscious striving towards the 'supra-personal', with the result that the 'general' will prevail over the 'personal'. Obedience, in this case, will be required not in relation to the human person, but as a subjection to the 'law', 'rule', 'function', 'institution', etc.[62]

A monk came to a contemporary elder Fr Paisy on Mt Athos and told him: 'Father, I have been made abbot of such and such monastery. Give me advice in how I should run the monastery'. Fr Paisy replied: 'Keep your monastery as disorganised as possible'. These words may seem unusual to those who see the monastic life primarily as a life of rigid discipline, strict rules and so on. However, there is great wisdom and experience behind these words.

There is a clear theological distinction between Gospel-type obedience and secular discipline, the two in fact constitute an antithesis to each other: discipline, as an impersonal element, may arrest the development of the hypostatic potential in man:

> Monastic obedience is a religious act, and, as such, it should be free, otherwise it would lose its religious significance … If in the monastery the abbot or other spiritual guides are obliged to use … 'discipline', it is a sure sign of the decline of monasticism, and perhaps even of the entire understanding of its goal and essence.[63]

When discipline prevails over Christian obedience, 'there is a possibility of the ultimate loss of the very aim of Christianity and the sense of life'.[64]

Elder Sophrony explains: 'A loss [of personal dimension in obedience] … cannot be redeemed by any external success of an institution or the perfection of the infrastructure of any impersonal "whole"'.[65] Thus, monastic obedience becomes an introduction into the trinitarian mode of being. It ensures the progress towards an art of communal existence, teaching how to love and to live with and, for another person, how to assimilate through love another person's will, mentality, aspirations, experiences,[66] becoming thereby 'the express-image of their hypostasis' (cf. Heb. 1:3). It facilitates the growth of the human person so as to extend its embrace to a universal scope, becoming a god-like centre that bears the whole of mankind in the heart as one's own life. Sophrony concludes: 'Progressing in obedience to God and to our neighbour we progress in love: we broaden our being … until we embrace the fullness of mankind.'[67] This universal unity finds its concrete expression within the monastic community where all are called to become one, as God is One. Above all it expresses itself in prayer: 'Everyone, bearing in his prayer all the members of the Community, strives to achieve what the commandment sets before us: "Thou shalt love thy neighbour as thyself" – that is, as "one's own" life'.[68]

In 1991 Colin Gunton published a remarkable book – *The Promise of the Trinitarian Theology*. One might hope that the ascetic communal principle that is so prominently stressed in Orthodox monastic spirituality, setting the Trinity as the ultimate rule of life of the monastic community, is also a promise, heralding far reaching implications. This principle 'The Trinity as our ascetic project' waits to be extended far beyond monastic life and to be applied to all units of human society, which is witnessing a rapid disintegration of communal life. Trinitarian asceticism can provide a rich source of inspiration, to family life above all, and then to all the strata of human communities: wherever there are inter-human relationships, there is a place to practise the Trinity.

Notes

1 Robin Parry, *Worshipping Trinity: Coming Back to the Heart of Worship* (Milton Keynes, UK: Paternoster, 2005), p. 17.
2 Peter Toon and James Spiceland, eds, introduction to *One God in Trinity* (London: Samuel Bagster, 1980), p. xi.
3 For an overview of the build-up of the ideal of humble love in Russian thinkers, see Nadezhda Gorodetsky, 'Acceptance of Humiliation as a National Ideal', in *The Humiliated Christ in Modern Russian Thought* (London: SPCK, 1938), pp. 1–74.
4 Bissarion Belinsky, *Collected Works* (in Russian), edited by Sergey A. Vengerov (St. Petersburg, 1900), vol. 1, p. 319.
5 See Murray Krieger, 'Dostoyevsky's "Idiot": The Curse of Saintliness', in *Dostoevsky: A Collection of Critical Essays*, edited by René Wellek (Englewood Cliffs, NJ: Prentice Hall, 1962), pp. 39–52.
6 See Richard Peace, *The Enigma of Gogol: An Examination of the Writings of N. V. Gogol and Their Place in the Russian Literary Tradition* (Cambridge: Cambridge University Press, 2009), pp. 2ff, 177ff, 263ff.
7 See Michael Meerson, introduction to *The Trinity of Love in Modern Russian Theology: The Love Paradigm and the Retrieval of Western Medieval Love Mysticism in Modern Russian Trinitarian Thought (From Solovyov to Bulgakov)* (Quincy, IL: Franciscan Press, 1998), p. xix.
8 See ibid., 21ff; cf. Teresa Obolevitch, 'All-unity according to V. Soloviev and S. Frank. A comparative analysis', *Forum Philosophicum* 15/2 (2010), pp. 413–25; Frederick Copleston, *Russian Religious Philosophy* (Wellwood: Search Press, 1988), pp. 62–5.
9 See Andrzej Walicki, *A History of Russian Thought: From the Enlightenment to Marxism* (Stanford, CA: Stanford University Press, 1979), pp. 105f.
10 Thomas Špidlík, *L'idée russe: une autre vision de l'homme* (Troyes: Editions Fates, 1994), p. 63.
11 Meerson, *The Trinity of Love*, p. xix.
12 Sergius Bulgakov, *The Lamb of God*, translated by Boris Jakim (Cambridge: William B. Eerdmans, 2008), pp. 113–14.
13 Sergius Bulgakov, *Unfading Light: Contemplations and Speculations*, translated and edited by Thomas Allan Smith (Cambridge: William B. Eerdmans, 2012), p. 292.
14 Meerson, *The Trinity of Love*, p. xix.
15 Sergius Bulgakov, 'St Sergius' Testament to the Russian Theology', *Put'* 5 (1926), p. 6 (in Russian).
16 See ibid., pp. 7–9.
17 Sergius Bulgakov, 'The Problem of Immortality', *Put'* 52 (1937), p. 22 (in Russian).
18 Špidlík, *L'idée*, pp. 63–7.
19 Meerson, *The Trinity of Love*, p. 119.
20 Pavel Florensky, *The Pillar and Ground of the Truth*, translated by Boris Jakim (Princeton, NJ: Princeton University Press, 1997), p. 64.
21 Meerson, *The Trinity of Love*, pp. 130–5.
22 Archimandrite Sophrony Sakharov, *Birth into a Kingdom Which Cannot Be Moved* (Moscow: The Monastery of St John the Baptist, 1999), p. 187 (in Russian).
23 Archimandrite Sophrony Sakharov, *La félicité de connaître la voie* (Genève: Labor & Fides, 1988), p. 16.
24 See David W. Faberberg, 'Antinomy in Pavel Florensky and Paradox in Gilbert Chesterton', *The Chesterton Review* 31:1/2 (2005) pp. 81–94.
25 Nicholas Sakharov, *I Love, Therefore I Am: The Theological Legacy of Archimandrite Sophrony* (Crestwood, NY: SVS, 2002), p. 15.

26 Archimandrite Sophrony, *We Shall See Him As He Is*, translated by Rosemary Edmonds (Tiptree, Essex: The Monastery of St John the Baptist, 1988), pp. 176, 217.

27 Archimandrite Sophony, *Félicité*, p. 30.

28 Archimandrite Sophrony, *The Struggle for Knowledge of God: Letters from Mt Athos to David Balfour* (Moscow: Palomnik, 2003), 270–71 (in Russian).

29 Archimandrite Sophrony, foreword to *Wisdom From Mount Athos: The Writings of Staretz Silouan 1866–1938*, translated by Rosemary Edmonds (Crestwood, NY: SVS, 1974), pp. 15–16.

30 For the trinitarian theology of Sergius Bulgakov, see Nikolai Sakharov, 'Essential Bulgakov: His Ideas about Sophia, the Trinity and Christ', *St. Vladimir's Theological Quarterly* 55:2 (2011), pp. 183ff.

31 See Andreas J. Köstenberger and Scott R. Swain, *Father, Son and Spirit: The Trinity and John's Gospel* (Downer's Grove: IVP, 2008).

32 Archimandrite Sophrony, *His Life is Mine*, translated by Rosemary Edmonds (Oxford: Mowbray, 1977), p. 43.

33 Archimandrite Sophrony, *Saint Silouan the Athonite*, translated by Rosemary Edmonds (East Kilbride: The Monastery of St John the Baptist, 1991), p. 47.

34 Sophrony, *Silouan the Athonite*, p. 372.

35 Sophrony, *The Struggle for Knowledge of God*, p. 250.

36 Sophrony, *His Life is Mine*, p. 29.

37 Ibid., p. 43.

38 Notably, it fails to feature in Mark Appold's *The Oneness Motif in the Fourth Gospel: Motif Analysis and Exegetical Probe into the Theology of John* (Tübingen: Mohr Siebeck, 1975).

39 For the patristic idea of disintegration (*phthora*) see Edwin Zackrison, *In the Loins of Adam: A Historical Study of Original Sin in Adventist Theology* (Bloomington, IN: iUniverse, 2004), p. 48.

40 On the patristic understanding of the fall and its aftermath see Zackrison, *In the Loins of Adam*, pp. 39–114; Ian A. McFarland, *In Adam's Fall: A Meditation on the Christian Doctrine of Original Sin* (Chichester: Wiley-Blackwell, 2010), pp. 29–116.

41 Archimandrite Sophrony, *Spiritual Homilies*, vol. 1 (Moscow: Palomnik, 2003), p. 223 (in Russian).

42 Walter E. Pilgrim, *Good News to the Poor: Wealth and Poverty in Luke* (Eugene, OR: Wipf & Stock, 2011), pp. 180–81.

43 Denise Tucker, *A Heart in Need of Repentance* (Bloomington, IN: Xlibris Corporation, 2012), p. 14.

44 Fernando Mendez-Moratalla, *The Paradigm of Conversion in Luke* (London: T&T Clark, 2004), p. 179.

45 Archimandrite Sophrony, *Birth into a Kingdom*, p. 187.

46 Michael Byrnes, *Conformation to the Death of Christ and the Hope of Resurrection* (Rome: Gregorian University Press 2003), p. 208; cf. Sam K. Williams, 'Again *Pistis Christou*', *Catholic Biblical Quarterly* 49 (1987), p. 446.

47 Archimandrite Sophrony, *Birth into a Kingdom*, p. 105.

48 See Stephen McDowell and Mark Beliles, *Liberating the Nations: Biblical Principles of Government, Education, & Politics* (Charlottesville, VA: Providence Foundation, 1995), p. 78.

49 See Harvey Diamond, *Sons and Servants: Real Identities Lost and Found* (Lincoln, NE: iUniverse, 2006), p. 178.

50 Sophrony, *Silouan the Athonite*, pp. 237–8.

51 Ibid., pp. 238–9.

52 See Sophrony, *We Shall See Him as He Is*, p. 97: 'St Silouan's method is to place us before the general principle and them leave us to work out and diagnose our own case.'

53 See Thomas J. Altizer, *Total Presence: The Language of Jesus and the Language of Today* (New York: Seabury, 1980), pp. 1–18.

54 Ibid., p. 55.
55 David Garrett Izzo, *W.H. Auden: a Legacy* (West Cornwall, CT: Locust Hill Press, 2002), p. 421.
56 On the Patristic concept of *perichoresis*, see Verna Harrison, 'Perichoresis in the Greek Fathers', *St Vladimir's Theological Quarterly* 35 (1991). pp. 53–65.
57 Vladimir Lossky, *In the Image and Likeness of God* (Crestwood, NY: SVS, 1974), p. 81.
58 Walter Kasper, *The God of Jesus Christ*, translated Matthew J. O'Connel (New York: Crossroad, 1984), pp. 288–9.
59 Meerson, *The Trinity of Love*, p. 185.
60 Sophrony, *Félicité*, p. 21.
61 Sophrony, *Birth into a Kingdom,* p. 191.
62 Ibid., p. 175.
63 Ibid., p. 141.
64 Ibid., p. 175.
65 Ibid., p. 175.
66 Ibid., pp. 174–5.
67 Ibid., p. 138.
68 Ibid., pp. 187–8.

Part 2

Personal accounts
of a theological life

4 Ecumenical confessions of an unconventional Protestant

Frances Young

Theology as a way of life

Asked to speak from my own ecclesial tradition, I can only respond by saying that among Methodists, especially at the grassroots level, theology is treated with a certain suspicion. It is no accident that Methodist theology has to be 'unmasked', to borrow from the title of the collection of papers on the matter,[1] though that in itself suggests that our theology is so embedded in our way of life that uncovering it takes a certain discernment. In Methodist conversation, at the annual conference and in committees at all levels, matters concerning mission and social action predominate (e.g. Mission Alongside the Poor, Fresh Expressions). Theology emerges either under ecumenical pressure (e.g. what about the *filioque?*) or in response to challenging and controversial issues (e.g. sexuality); and when it does, debates generally crystallize around appropriate appeal to scripture.

The practice of the presence of God

Methodists tend to be active rather than contemplative: we don't practise the presence of God, we acknowledge it or pray for it, seeking to ground an essentially pragmatic way of life in worship and private devotion. We look for 'scriptural holiness', not in those who withdraw from the world, but those who engage with it. So it is hardly surprising how often I have felt I should be doing some good in the world, instead of being a theologian. Indeed, there is resistance to Quietism and a bit of a Pelagian tendency in our tradition, though it is always counterbalanced by the evangelical sense that God's salvation in Christ is sheer gift, to be received with thanksgiving through the means of grace. Even if it *is* all sheer gift, including the sense of God's presence, you won't, of course, get it if you don't put yourself in a position to receive it; and while it is all too easy for the means of grace to become routinized, faithful attention to those means of grace ensures the possibility of knowing oneself held in God's reality, caught up in love and thanksgiving, and also by being able to carry over a sense of God's presence into the everyday living of one's life.

So, what are those means of grace for Methodists? This term tends to be associated with the sacraments, and it is not always remembered that, a century or more before the Oxford Movement, Methodism was itself a sacramental movement within the Church of England; Charles Wesley's remarkable Eucharistic hymns are a particular legacy of that fact. For some Methodists, Holy Communion remains a highlight, made all the more so perhaps by less frequent practice – in general, just once a month or on special occasions. But Methodists know other means of grace: preaching of the Word, hymn singing, fellowship groups, covenant services, Bible reading and private prayer, and, to use rather traditional language, self-denial and 'works of mercy'. The earliest Methodists got their name from the methodical pursuit of a rule of life that could produce growth in discipleship and in the practice of holiness. I, myself, have argued more than once that John Wesley democratized the ancient monastic ideals of the Macarian homilies, in which he identified an essentially scriptural understanding of the struggle for perfection. Methodism has always proclaimed the possibility of transformation, of new birth through the Spirit and by God's love. Our way of life embraces both an inner life and practical action, both personal commitment and social engagement. I suppose that that is our equivalent to practising the presence of God, though the phrase would seem a little alien to most Methodists, as would calling our way of life 'theology'.

Ecumenical confessions of an unconventional Protestant

Why should I choose to write about that? I will take three key themes and explain something of my quirky personal journey as theologian, which has been formed, but not constrained, by Methodism.

Scripture

The Methodist household in which I grew up was involved in education – my father was a distinguished headmaster, my mother a maths teacher, both were children of the manse. Though I dislike the label, if used we would have been described as liberal, not fundamentalist. Yet, the Bible was inescapable. John Wesley claimed to be a man of one book, and the Protestant *sola scriptura* is embedded in our tradition. I vividly remember, as a young teenager, doing scripture exams on Ezra and Nehemiah, of all things, not at school, but through church. So, maybe it is not so surprising that as a Classics student at University, I suddenly found I needed to use my Greek for New Testament study, inspired by reading the *Commentary on John* by a great Methodist scholar, Kingsley Barrett. It is no accident, by the way, that Methodists have made a more distinguished mark in biblical studies than in other aspects of theology.

Daily snippets of the Bible, usually with notes to help to understand them, constitute the regular diet of devout Methodists and are used in their Quiet time to enable prayer and reflection. Once the Bible became my profession, I found that practice to be unsustainable. Respectable scholarship then meant that the Bible had to be treated as a historical document, to be set in its original context, and studied in the original languages, Hebrew and Greek, if its witness to God's saving events in history were to be properly understood. I was educated in biblical criticism in the period during which there was extreme scepticism as to whether the historian could be sure about the authenticity of any of the words and deeds of Jesus recorded in the Gospels. Back then, as a Methodist lay preacher interpreting scripture in the context of church worship, I found I couldn't preach from the Gospels, given that one of my core values is integrity and I was intellectually uncertain what I could and could not accept as 'fact'. I was still less able to ground prayer in contextless biblical snippets. So a prayerful sense of God's presence was not facilitated by the conventional practices with which I had grown up.

So, what has rescued the Bible for me as a means of grace? At the intellectual level, shifts in hermeneutics and my own studies in the exegesis of the church fathers have made a profound difference. But, at a deeper level, it is been gifts arising from ecumenical encounters. The first and most fundamental of those gifts has been a renewed capacity to read myself/ourselves into the story – which is of course what my Methodist forebears have done unthinkingly for generations – but God gave it back to me in other ways. The local convent invited neighbours to a carol service; I took my severely disabled son in his buggy. For the first time ever I found myself in the presence of a life-size Mary, and afterwards by the time I had reached my front gate, this poem had formed itself in my mind:[2]

> *Mary, my child's lovely.*
> *Is yours lovely too?*
> *Little hands, little feet,*
> *Curly hair, smiles sweet.*
>
> *Mary, my child's broken.*
> *Is yours broken too?*
> *Crushed by affliction,*
> *Hurt by rejection,*
> *Disfigured, stricken,*
> *Silent submission.*
>
> *Mary, my heart's bursting.*
> *Is yours bursting too?*
> *Bursting with labour, travail and pain.*
> *Bursting with agony, ecstasy, gain.*
> *Bursting with sympathy, anger, compassion.*
> *Bursting with praising Love's transfiguration.*
>
> *Mary, my heart's joyful.*
> *Is yours joyful too?*

I could offer many other examples, but the importance of this kind of reading has been reinforced, first, by the 'faith-sharing' practice I have met in the context of *L'Arche*: a scriptural passage is read together in a small group, and then each person shares what it meant to them personally – exactly what my Methodist forebears did in their class meetings; and secondly, by recognition that in the preaching of the fathers this 'typology', in which correlations were made between themselves and biblical characters, was what drew people into the biblical stories in the early church. If we are ecumenical over time, we can rediscover how people's lives and their understanding of themselves have been shaped by the biblical material.

Common lectionary

The second gift has been the common lectionary – an ecumenical achievement, not always valued in my tradition, but, for me, a discipline and a resource, particularly since my ordination, as week by week I have found myself reading side by side selections from the Old Testament, the epistles and the Gospels, often in new configurations, and been challenged to see what holds them together and addresses a 'word' for the next Sunday's congregation. Again, this process has been reinforced by my reading of the fathers, for whom two things were vital to scriptural interpretation: (1) constant cross-reference across all the biblical texts to see how one would illuminate another and lead on to deeper meanings; and (2) a sense of the whole story from creation, through the fall, then redemption by means of the incarnation of the Son of God, to the end, the fulfilment of God's purposes, anticipated by new creation in Christ.[3]

So, I have become an unconventional Protestant in the sense that the 'plain meaning' of any given scriptural text is not enough from me. Ecumenical perspectives and the sense of Christian identity over much longer trajectories than my own Methodist tradition have not only significantly enlarged my approach, opening up the possibility of multiple readings in different circumstances, but also enabled the reclamation of elements of my own tradition, once rejected because of the naivety so often evident in actual practice. But I remain deeply Protestant in my commitment to preaching the Word, and I regret the incipient passing over of that great tradition, as our culture demands visuals and sound-bites, and people's limited attention-spans deter speakers from attempting to engage people in the spiritual drama that scripture offers. For it is through great preaching that people are caught up into something bigger than themselves, and the fundamental aim of scripture – to transform – is made effective in people's lives, and God's presence made real for those who have ears to hear.

I regret too the passing of the great tradition of extemporary prayer. Masters of the art, versed in the resonant phrases of the King James Version, could evoke the presence of God and carry a congregation into the beyond. They embodied the grounding of prayer in scripture. Of course, extemporary prayer is always a risk – it so easily descends into the shoddy, the banal, uninspired routine habits of language and intonation. The liturgical movement has given us, along with our ecumenical partners, more of a shared language, and has encouraged the use of written or prepared prayers, but reading prayers becomes routine even more easily. Taking the risk of voicing extemporary prayer can enable it to become a gift, a gift of the unexpected. And, what our Methodist tradition should surely foster again is praying that emerges from pondering scripture, from listening to what God has to say to us.

This takes us to the traditional Methodist practice of private devotion, the Quiet time, with scripture at the start, then lists of concerns to pray for, often assisted by the Prayer Handbook, published year by year – a wonderful discipline which broke down my difficulty with scripture which was compounded by a youthful suspicion of pious practices. I have tried out various alternatives. For a time I prayed my way through the Psalter day by day – a centuries – old practice. At one stage I came across a little book about long wandering prayer – just going for a walk, and allowing everything and everyone you meet to trigger prayer. Long wandering prayers happen for me when travelling, walking, cycling, but most often in bed in the dark when sleep eludes me. This may seem undisciplined, yet it symbolizes something about God relating to the whole of life, which is what Methodism has always been about: 'praying with the Bible and the newspaper side by side' is one popular way of putting it. I'm still searching and remain frustrated often. Yet, I'm learning not to flagellate myself because, in the end, prayer is never an achievement but rather a gift, and my spiritual helpmate insists that my work is my prayer. Yes indeed – for the gift comes from a constant attempt to cultivate a habit of mind which sees everything in the light of God, God's blessing, God's love; through my reading, thinking and writing, I find myself receiving remarkable insights which do indeed make God present – truly theology is my way of life. And, once again, it is through ecumenical contacts that I have been able to reclaim my own Methodist tradition of finding God anytime, anywhere; through *L'Arche* and Jean Vanier, learning to encounter God's presence in everyday, ordinary domestic activities, caring and sharing with people who have profound disabilities, receiving and giving in mutual reciprocity, my heart leaping as my son chuckles and smiles, or turning to God in helplessness when he's distressed, re-learning my own frailty and dependence. Jean Vanier once said, '[Your son,] Arthur is your gateway to God'.

Fellowship and communion

John Wesley insisted that no one could be a Christian on their own, and from the beginning he encouraged small groups or classes to meet regularly for prayer and Bible study and to offer mutual support, not least by sharing testimonies about the way God had been present in their lives, or spoken through scripture, since last they met. Finding the presence of God, being enabled to hear what God has to say to us, comes through relationships with other people, through fellowship – that is deeply ingrained in the Methodist tradition. It was part of my student experience in MethSoc groups at University, in which we studied and prayed and played together, discovering deep friendships there. In later life, however, ecumenical groups have meant most. A long-term local ecumenical group was the context in which each shared their personal pilgrimage and it was through that process that God was made real to me again after years of anxious doubt, triggered by the birth of my profoundly disabled son, Arthur. Small, short-term ecumenical and international groups at gatherings of *Faith and Light* or *L'Arche* have given me extraordinary gifts of grace – literally, the gift of this beautiful, little hand-carved 'holding cross' – something to which I simply cling when prayer seems beyond me. One of the most wonderful groups consisted of eight people charged with being an international ecumenical commission for *Faith and Light*: two Roman Catholics, two Orthodox, two Anglicans, two Methodists, hailing from Argentina, Northern Ireland, Moscow, Syria, the USA, Britain and Zimbabwe. We met annually for several days and became profoundly knitted together in work and prayer, discovering the richness of the body of Christ when difference is taken up and transformed through love and sharing.

One of the characteristics of the Methodist tradition is giving expression to this reality at the communion table. Our custom is to gather in groups to receive, not to kneel as private individuals, but for each group to share and then be dismissed with a blessing. This is a sign that we belong together in the body of Christ, and together we participate in Christ with a great cloud of witnesses. And, in such a context may come the gift of God's presence and love, an overwhelming sense that somehow you are receiving, on behalf of others, people you care for deeply but who cannot, for whatever reason, receive the communion for themselves.

I suppose it is this core sense of communion with one another in Christ that makes it so painful not to be included, unable to receive the Eucharistic elements with others to whom one has become very close through ecumenical fellowship. John Wesley called the Eucharist a 'converting ordinance' – so we Methodists invite all those who love the Lord Jesus, or who seek to love him, to join us at his table. Even in ecumenical settings, if I'm presiding at communion, I issue that invitation and some have responded, even if they should not according to the canonical rules of their church. For us Methodists, it is indeed *his* table, the table already laid, to which Christ invites us (traditionally we make no offertory of bread and wine, though some Methodists do now follow that practice through ecumenical influence). As the Wesleyan hymn puts it, 'His presence makes the feast', and a feast is shared together, enabling transcendence of our human differences. I have a vivid recollection of experiencing exactly this at an inner-city church when in training for ordination. For the first time I was involved in the distribution of communion. Gathered in the congregation was a cross-section of society, young and old, black and white, people with a high degree of competence, people with disabilities or unemployed – their lives reflected in their outstretched hands, smooth, rough, clean, dirt-stained – and someone took the initiative to push my son's wheelchair up to join in and receive a blessing. There and then it was as if I saw the Lord, high and lifted up in the midst of the Temple.

Hymn-singing

Growing up a Methodist I first sensed the presence of God when singing hymns. It is no accident that Methodists have put the hymn book alongside the Bible in private prayer; what we might call 'our theology' is enshrined particularly in Wesley's poetry. But, it is the physical act of communal singing which enables a kind of ecstasy, of being taken up into something bigger than oneself, yet being so profoundly affirmed and loved that self-concern drops away and love spills over onto others and into the world. The physicality is important – when I was younger and fitter, God's presence often overtook me as I ran a mile around the local block under the stars; I understand why dance has so often been a core element in human religious rites. For me, music has always fuelled a sense of self-transcendence, from hymn singing to oratorios – Protestant classics like Handel's *Messiah*, Bach's *St Matthew Passion*, Brahms' *German Requiem*, then, more ecumenically, Haydn's *Creation*, the great masses and requiems, Mozart, Verdi. But, not just overtly religious music: I have had a sense of the presence of God at secular classical concerts in Birmingham Symphony Hall as often as in church. But I have also learned to swing my body to the beat of black Pentecostal choruses, to find deep stillness in Anglican cathedral music, to be transported by Russian Orthodox chants, to join the procession in Lourdes singing *Ave Maria*. Such are the ecumenical confessions of an unconventional Protestant.

But, perhaps even more extraordinary, is the way ecumenical involvements have enabled my senses to expand, from hearing to seeing. With an artist friend I once noticed how, together in a wood, she looked, while I closed my eyes and listened. Yet increasingly my eyes have been opened and it is through two Coptic icons that I have found a deeper relationship with Jesus and profound inner healing.

Notes

1 Clive Marsh, Brian Beck, Angela Shier-Jones and Helen Wareing, eds, *Unmasking Methodist Theology* (London and New York: Continuum, 2004).
2 First published in *Face to Face* (London: Epworth, 1985), and many times since!
3 See further *God's Presence: A Contemporary Recapitulation of Early Christianity* (Cambridge: Cambridge University Press, 2013).

5 Augustine on practicing the presence of God

Margaret R. Miles

I.

My paperback copy of Rex Warner's translation of Augustine's *Confessions*, which I first read in 1964, is so tattered that I carry it around in a cut-to-fit box. When I open it a small shower of confetti, from its dry and brittle pages, litters the floor. Over the last forty-five years, I have re-read St. Augustine's *Confessions* every few years, in English and in Latin, astonished that reading the same text, having new experience and questions, made a different text pop into my eyes. Each time I read it I notice themes, preoccupations and habits of mind – Augustine's and my own – that I had not noticed before.

Augustine's *Confessions* is good to think with. In my book, *Augustine and the Fundamentalist's Daughter*, I think with the *Confessions* as Augustine thought with scripture. I seek to identify the intellectual and emotional events and ideas that were as formative for me as his were for him. I seek to emulate the rigour and depth with which Augustine thought about his life. Above all, I seek to understand Augustine's advice on how to practice the presence of God.

II.

My conversation with Augustine is insistently first-personal. He did not offer a manual, a 'how to', in a one-size-fits-all sense. He 'talked about' his own practice of God's presence. Similarly, I describe how *I* came, over many years, to understand Augustine's reflections, not solely with my rational mind, but with my life. A few remarks on method are necessary to that end.

There is plenty of precedent for first-personal approaches to understanding. In addition to Augustine's example, many centuries later, no less an author than Descartes, the so-called 'Father of Rationalism', said that he did not present his *Discourse on the Method* as *the method* for general understanding. He wrote: 'My aim here is not to teach *the* method that each person should follow in order to conduct his reason well, but solely to show in what way I have tried to conduct my own'. His method, he said, was *not* for the purpose of understanding '*what can be known*, but what *I* can know'.[1] In a letter to a friend, Descartes further explained that he called his writing a discourse, rather than a treatise, because his aim 'was not to teach, but only to talk about it'.[2] In kindred spirits, more than a thousand years before Descartes, Augustine 'talked about' his experience of practicing the presence of God.

It seems to me that many scholars would like to bring our academic work and our life experience into a more explicit conversation. We don't know how, though; we have been trained, for centuries, to be 'objective' and we have learned to exclude ourselves, our particular experience, our particular training, our social location, race, and gender from our interpretation of texts. But the stubborn, urgent collection of selves each of us *is*, belligerently and inevitably enters our interpretations. Simply stated, the choice we have is whether to acknowledge, or to attempt to mask, the autobiographies we bring to thinking about ideas and texts, the lenses through which I interpret Augustine on prasticing the presence of God.

Moreover, the autobiographies we bring to interpreting the texts and the events that we study consist not only of our intellectual resources and habits. We academics have had to *learn* to think with our heads – with our heads only – and we are proud of our ability to exclude body, feelings, interests, longings, and desires from our thinking activity. It has come to seem self-evident that this is the *right* way to think. From the practice of thinking with our heads only – we have developed the assumption that rationality is the opposite of, and is opposed to, feeling and emotion.

Moreover, if we are to be able to think more rigorously, that is, more honestly, we need a different model of 'person' than Western philosophers and theologians have assumed. We usually imagine 'persons' as compositions, *components* of body and mind or soul and spirit. We have reached no consensus on our components. But, when we analyse 'person', as assembled components, we lose the person.[3] To assume Descartes's separable mind and body, uneasily and hierarchically stacked, is to distort and undermine who we most fundamentally are. For a person is, irreducibly one entity, an 'intelligent body'.

Because we have read Augustine attending only to the language of body and soul that he inherited from his intellectual culture, we have not noticed an alternative construction of 'person' that permeates his *Confessions*. Throughout, Augustine described strong physical and emotional feelings that prompted and informed intellectual understandings. Perhaps the most famous of these narrations was his description of the intellectual and emotional crisis surrounding his famous conversion in the garden at Ostia:

> My forehead, cheeks, eyes, colour of face, and inflection of voice expressed my mind better than the words I used … [I] made many movements of my body … I tore my hair, beat my forehead, locked my fingers together, clasped my knee … flung myself down on the ground somehow under a fig tree and gave free rein to my tears (*Confessions* 8. 8, 12).

For Augustine, new understandings were simultaneously intellectual, emotional, *and* physical events. Even while he used the language of 'body' and 'soul', what he *described* was an intelligent body. He said, recalling his youthful excitement, in reading Cicero's *Hortensius*, that the treatise '*altered my way of feeling*' (3.4).

'When music was difficult to find, it was very powerful', wrote the novelist Arthur Phillips.[4] The same could be said for books. 'Where can I find the books?'[5] Augustine moaned. Books, the right books, are perhaps perennially difficult to find. 'I was on fire', Augustine wrote about his reading of the *Hortensius* – not too strong a description of my own avid reading. Later I learned to be critical of books, to read suspiciously, asking how authors' perspectives and interests directed their texts. I learned to notice what is *not* in the text, as well as what *is* there. I wanted to read Augustine's *Confessions* both sympathetically *and* critically, a difficult feat certainly. We mostly read authors who interpret *either* sympathetically, ignoring critical questions, *or* critically, sweeping anything in the text that is beautiful, moving, or illuminating into a negative interpretation. I found that reading Augustine in the context of his life, the details of which he provided more generously than any other author of his time, and interpreting him in the context of my life, enabled a more-or-less simultaneous sympathetic and critical reading, a *conversation*.

Allowing myself, even briefly, to see the world as Augustine saw it has been a life-changing experience. The passionate, even violent, imagery with which he described his search for God challenges all sluggishness. Yet for Augustine, the resolution of his anguished search was more like relaxing than it was like a struggle: '*Cessavi de me paululum*' – 'I relaxed a little from myself', he wrote (*Confessions* 7.14). Augustine's rhythm of avid search and grateful acceptance has become the rhythm of my own life.

III.

I was born into, and grew up in, the home of a fundamentalist Baptist minister. Dad's father, a farmer in Eastern Ontario, Canada, became wealthy – 'the Lord blessed him', as he put it – for growing strawberries in rich soil in which everyone else grew tobacco. When he died, his money went to 'the missionaries'. Dad's people were simple rural people with few wants, generous spirits, and ungrammatical English. Dad left the farm, went to the city, and became a speech teacher and a preacher. He prided himself on his flawless English; he read the dictionary in search of interesting words. Over his desk hung a plaque that read 'Thy speech maketh thee known' (Matthew 26:73). He corrected his children's speech constantly. On a visit home, after I had been teaching at Harvard for several years, he corrected one of my sentences remarking: 'You have been among people who damaged your grammar'. (As I recall, the issue was whether to use 'which' or 'that' in my sentence.)

My father's fundamentalism, founded on his passionate love for God and scripture, was most evident when he preached. With his well-thumbed-through and red-underlined Bible in hand, he clearly relished exploration and interpretation of 'God's word' (in the King James version). His delight was palpable and communicable. Dad's capacity for rich delight was his greatest gift to me. When I felt myself immersed in, and excited by, the beauty of the texts I was teaching, I recognized that this ability to lose himself in delight was what he experienced in preaching.[6]

Confident that he accurately apprehended God's character and commands, my father pursued his mission with persistence and fervour. To neglect to point sinners to God at every opportunity would have been, in his view, the most reprehensible cowardice and laziness. Repeatedly throughout his life, people complained of his aggressive 'witnessing'. To Dad, these complaints demonstrated simply that one who does 'the Lord's work' can expect the Devil to use every possible means to undermine, harm, and attempt to destroy him.

While he was on a rare vacation in Hawaii, someone remarked to him in a friendly way, 'Hot as hell today, isn't it!' Father replied sternly, 'Young man, I hope you never find out how hot hell is!'

American Christian fundamentalism, as I experienced it as a child, was more than a set of beliefs, more than the insistence that every word of scripture came from the mouth of God. Fundamentalism was also a worldview, an acute alertness to wrongdoing, and a particular construction and understanding of 'self'. The fundamentalist self begins with an especially poignant sense of lack, 'I am a sinner'.

No one described the experience of the sinful self better than Augustine did. Multiple vivid images and metaphors describe his sense of desperation and evisceration: malnutrition, insomnia, itching wounds and scratched scabs, and the feeling of being wasted and scattered, distracted and dispersed:

> For I have been spilled and scattered among times whose order I do not know; my thoughts, the innermost bowels of my soul, are torn apart with the crowding tumults of variety. And so it will be, he added, until all together I can flow into you, purified and molten by the fire of your love. And I shall stand and become set in you, in my mold, in your truth (11.29).

Augustine grounded the self in a personal God who, by watching him and *watching out* for him, guaranteed his reality.

My parents personalized the universe as Augustine did. They understood that everything that happened to them was ordered by a personal God. Nothing was coincidental or accidental. They considered scripture to be God's direct communication to them in the particular circumstances of their lives. Augustine interpreted a painful toothache as God torturing him to remind him of his sins (9.4). Generations of Christians have comforted themselves with the belief that God allows nothing to happen that is too much for them to bear.[7] They then trustingly proceed to bear whatever needs to be borne, understanding the pains and distresses that come to them either as God's punishment or as tests of their faith.

Augustine exemplified the fundamentalist's obsessive fretting over his relationship with God. He was fascinated by restlessness and rest (1.1), by anxiety and relaxation (7.14), because he had so little of the latter. His passionate nature easily gave way to compulsive self-doubt and relentless pursuit, whether of honours, marriage, money (6.6) or of God. Relaxation was, for Augustine, always temporary, a momentary relief that prepared him for the next onslaught of anxiety. Even his conversion did not alter his intense anxiety; the later books of the *Confessions* still fester over minutiae that seemed to him to threaten his relationship with God; he still exhibited intemperate distress over such abstract matters as how to explain time (11.22).[8]

Focused on the individual and his relationship with God, both Augustine and the fundamentalists of my childhood failed to address social sins. My fundamentalists were concerned with individual sins – sexual temptations, lying, neglecting to read scripture and praying on a daily basis, etc. Similarly, Augustine did not worry about the sins of his society – slavery, poverty, military aggression; he considered these to be inevitable and necessary social evils. Nor did my immigrant parents worry about social evils – poverty, war, inadequate medical care, grossly unjust distribution of wealth, and failure to provide safety nets for the young, the old, the poor, and the marginalized.

At this point, a caveat is necessary: Not all fundamentalists are alike. I know people who hold fundamentalist religious beliefs, but who are more loving than they are judgmental, more accepting of others whose beliefs differ from their own than my father, and who experience more joy than was characteristic of my home. My intent is not to demonstrate that Augustine was a fundamentalist in any contemporary sense of that label. While Augustine's *Confessions* demonstrate a number of fundamentalist traits, Augustine and my father did not have identical, or even similar, psyches.

One of the most important differences is Augustine's attitude toward scriptural interpretation. He found great relief in Ambrose's advice that scripture is not to be taken literally; instead, the spiritual meaning must be sought. Moreover, Augustine professed to tolerate, even to appreciate, multiple interpretations of scripture, as long, he said, as they did not violate Christian doctrine. He wrote:

> Can you not see how foolish it is out of all that abundance of perfectly true meanings which can be extracted from those words rashly to assert that one particular meaning was the one that Moses had chiefly in mind, and thereby in one's pernicious quarrelsomeness to offend charity herself? (12.25)

What? Multiple interpretations of scripture?! For my father, there was a right way – his, and a wrong way – yours.

IV.

For much of my life I have been occupied with an urgent and strenuous effort to come to terms with the fundamentalist psyche that I inherited. Altering my beliefs was easy compared to changing my assumptions about myself, other people, and the world. Even more difficult to identify and modify were those habits of mind and behaviour. In some significant ways, I am still a fundamentalist. For example, I retain a certain suspicion of American society – its social arrangements, media, and consumer orientation – a suspicion that is highly reminiscent of my parents' religious and immigrant perspective. But, most importantly, I sought to change my beliefs and values without losing my father's passion.

Gradually, I learned, as Augustine put it, to 'relax a little from myself' ('*cessavi de me paululum*' 7.14). Indeed, I continue to find that life offers abundant opportunities for getting over oneself. The earliest experience of this that I recall occurred when I was two. A snapshot shows me sitting on a feeding trough among chickens on my grandfather Miles's farm in eastern Ontario, Canada. I look relaxed, leaning my chubby arms on my spread knees. My grandfather had a large, fenced chicken yard. When he brought me into the pen, the chickens, disturbed by our arrival, rose into the air to about my (2-year-old) height, in my face, frantically squawking, shedding feathers and raising clouds of dust. I was terrified. On the day the snapshot was taken, Grandpa told me that if, after entering the pen, I would be still for a minute so that the chickens would settle down and resume their pecking in the dust. I did so, and the feeling of triumph over my terror was tremendous.

That episode became a model for me of how to act when overwhelmed by noise and dust in whatever form. When I gave my interview lecture (in 1977) at Harvard, for example, I feared the moments after my lecture when I anticipated that all those intelligent and learned people would attack, disprove, and demolish my thesis most of all. But, I remembered the chickens and I invited several questions and observations before responding to those that intrigued me. Sure enough, the noise and dust settled quickly – the questions were not unfriendly after all – and there was a lively and helpful exchange. Thanks to the chickens!

V.

Moreover, I learned from Augustine to take beauty seriously. One of the many conversions Augustine described in his *Confessions* was to the *significance* of the natural world. He called God 'beauty so old and so new' ('*pulchritude tam antiqua et tam nova*' 10.27) and he reached this insight inductively, from attentiveness to the natural world.

> And what is this God? I asked the earth and it answered: 'I am not he', and all things that are on the earth confessed the same. I asked the sea and the deeps and the creeping things with living souls, and they replied: 'We are not your God.' ... And I said to all these things that lie about the gates of our senses, 'Tell me about my God. Tell me something about him.' And they cried out in a loud voice: 'He made us.' My question was in my contemplation of them, and their answer was in their beauty (10.6).

Augustine insisted that when a person contemplates visible beauty *with the right question* – 'tell me about my God' – natural beauty becomes evident. Until then it just *is what it is* – to paraphrase Paul Simon, the natural world can be either 'so beautiful or so what.'

My father's version of Augustine's inference from the natural world was this: Whenever I visited home as an adult Dad showed me his garden, plant by plant. At some point in the tour, overwhelmed by the beauty of the flowers and vegetables, he remarked scornfully, 'And they say there is no God!'

Is it possible to forego the fundamentalist's need for a personalized universe and yet retain the passion that my father had as he preached? I believe that it is. And is it possible to be both passionate and generous? Yes. For me the key to a generous passion was conversion to beauty. At first, when I took my little children to the beach, the large rhythm of the ocean waves calmed my body and mind. 'All right!' I said to myself, here is a large clue. If I can develop and refine my ability to experience the beauty of the world, I will understand something fundamental and substantial about the universe. The gift, the provision, the providence, is not health, wealth, perfect relationships or fame. It is beauty. So, I asked, can I become a person who *perceives beauty*, not as intellectual or aesthetic judgment, but *at the level of perception*?

I began to notice that the practice of noticing beauty was accompanied, inevitably, by a certain emotional state, an overwhelming feeling of gratitude.[9] Perhaps this feeling of gratitude is what such strange bedfellows as Plotinus,[10] Calvin, and Wittgenstein described as a strong feeling of the 'perfect safety of the universe', a sudden feeling of relaxation and gratitude.

VI. On practising the presence of God

'*Pondus meum, amor meus*' – 'my weight is my love' – Augustine said.[11] I think that this is not a simple descriptive statement. Instead, it is the claim that commitment to – not the *feeling*, but the *practice* of – love *is* to practise the presence of God. Ah, but so little of what media culture calls 'love' *is* love. Freud would alter Augustine's statement to '*pondeus meum, timor meus*' – 'my weight is my fear'. In pressing difficulties a person acts one way if fear dominates and motivates, another if love is the primary stimulus. To say, as Augustine did, 'My weight is my love', is to claim that one participates in the love that Christians call 'God', without an admixture of fear.

When my son was four, we visited my parents. Checking to see whether, as he suspected, I was not bringing my children up properly, Dad asked Ric whether he loved Jesus. Ric, bewildered, looked at me and replied, 'I love Mommy.' A perfect Augustinian answer! Augustine, quoting 1 John 4:16, said that because 'God *is* love', anyone who loves participates in God-who-is-love. But, alas, this was not the right answer for my father!

Karl Barth, who wrote thirteen volumes of neo-orthodox systematic theology, was once asked by a reporter whether he could describe his theology in one sentence. Barth said yes: 'Jesus loves me, this I know, for the Bible tells me so.' The reporter thought he was joking; he wasn't. The children's song, 'Jesus loves me, this I know', was the first thing I was taught about God; it was the first song I laboured to play with my chubby fingers on my three-quarter-sized violin as a four-year-old. It is very powerful and poignant to me that the first thing my sisters and I learned as little children is, according to both Augustine *and* an important twentieth-century theologian, the very essence of theology. The (often) counter-experiential and counter-cultural confidence that there is a loving heart in the universe and that I share in the rich circulation of love is precisely the truth and faith one needs for life. Commenting on 'God is love' (I John 4.16) in a sermon, Augustine said, in effect, and that is all you need to know about God.[12]

In my experience, *carrying over* psychic 'weight' from fear to love is the project of a lifetime. This, *this project* defined for Augustine practising the presence of God. Even if the goal cannot be fully achieved, there is significant progress in articulating the project with clarity. Once this 'spelling out' has been done, one can begin to weave the *project* of love into the large and small decisions of everyday life.[13] Augustine's *Confessions* traces his movement from the extreme anxiety that made him clutch at everything that crossed his path in the fear that something would be missed, to '*my weight is my love*'.

Notes

1 Discourse, 1.4. The title is 'Discours de la Méthode pour bien conduire sa raison et chercher la vérité dans les sciences'; Bernard Williams, *Descartes: The Project of Pure Enquiry* (New York: Penguin Books, 1978), p. 18, note 4.

2 Ibid.

3 Maxine Sheets Johnston, *The Corporeal Turn: An Interdisciplinary Reader* (Exeter: Imprint Academic, 2009), p. 20.

4 Arthur Phillips, *Prague* (New York: Random House, 2002), p. 294.

5 *Confessions* 6.11.

6 Exodus 34:29.

7 Tony Morrison, *Jazz* (New York: Alfred Knopf, 1992), p. 99: '"He ain't give you nothing you can't bear, Rose." But had He? Maybe this one time He had. Had misjudged and misunderstood her particular backbone. This one time. Her particular spine."'

8 'My soul is on fire to solve this very complicated enigma ... let my longing penetrate into these things ... Grant me what I love; for I do love it and it was you who granted me to love ... By Christ, I beg you, in his name, the holy of holies, let no one disturb me' (11.22). It is striking that this impassioned outburst occurs in Augustine's description of his struggle to understand time, a topic that, by his own admission, he did not need to understand: What, then, is time? I know what it is if no one asks me what it is, but if I want to explain it to someone who has asked me, I find that I do not know (11.14).

9 Meister Eckhart said, 'If the only prayer you say in your life is thank you, that would suffice.'

10 Plotinus, *Ennead* 3.4.4.

11 *Confessions* 13. 9.

12 Augustine, Homily on 1 John 4.4: 'If this were the one and only thing we heard from the voice of God's Spirit – "for God is love" – we should ask for nothing more'; Augustine: *Later Works*, edited by John Burnaby (Philadelphia: Westminster Press, 1955), p. 336.
13 Herbert Fingarette, *Self-Deception*, second edition (Berkeley: University of California Press, 2000), p. 39.

Part 3

Theological and liturgical retrievals

6 The liturgy, icons and the prayer of the heart

Andrew Louth

I am not sure that the 'practice of the presence of God' is a very natural Orthodox term, though the idea, central to Brother Laurence's book with that same title (from what I can remember of it), of living so that, whether in the kitchen or kneeling before the Blessed Sacrament, the sense of God's presence is palpable, certainly is. The phrase, 'the practice of the presence of God', suggests to my ears at least, some kind of technique, and right at the beginning of our study day, as we embarked on a period of silence, Martin Laird suggested various techniques of keeping in the silence of prayer: he mentioned praying short prayers such as the Jesus Prayer, the use of a prayer-rope, attention to breathing – all practices associated with what has come to be called 'hesychast prayer', characteristic of Orthodox monasticism, though these practices have spread well beyond the cloister. I might have taken that cue, and talked about the Jesus Prayer, and the practices associated with it, or about icons, which have also become much used in the West over the last few decades as a focus for meditative prayer. However, if I had done that directly, I am not sure that I would have given you much of an Orthodox perspective, for within the practice of Orthodoxy, the Jesus Prayer, or icons, is not a detachable practice or devotional item; within Orthodoxy they fit into the whole pattern of Orthodox life. Detached, they can take on another meaning, not unrelated to what they mean in Orthodox practice, but not the same; indeed, it seems to me that this has happened. I don't see this as a problem necessarily: what others take from Orthodox practice should be seen as a gift, and one doesn't seek to control the use others make of gifts they have been given. Nevertheless, these practices had their place in their original context, a context in which the notion of the presence of God is conceived rather differently, so much so, that an expression such as 'practice of the presence of God' no longer seems very natural.

It seems to me that any truly Orthodox spirituality – or indeed, theology – has to be seen as being rooted in the liturgy, by which I mean both the prayer of the Church, in its daily, weekly and yearly cycles, and what we call the 'Divine Liturgy', that is, the celebration of the Eucharist. What does this mean? Let me try and answer that by looking at what we *do*, for the Divine Liturgy is, above all, an action, rather than something said or sung.

The Divine Liturgy (and indeed other major services, for example, most of the sacraments, Baptism for instance, and the Vigil Service or, when celebrated separately, Matins) begins with the priest censing the holy table within the sanctuary or altar, and the whole sanctuary, and then coming out through the icon screen into the nave of the church to cense the church and the people by going round the church (usually clockwise) and finally returning, behind the iconostasis, to the altar again. This circular movement is repeated in the service, both literally in the later censings of the church, and also metaphorically in the repetition of the litanies, sometimes beginning 'Again and again in peace let us pray to the Lord' – the repetition picking up the cyclical sense of the liturgical action. The meaning of this cyclical movement can be unfolded in a number of ways. The author of the *Corpus Areopagiticum*, who wrote under the title of Dionysius the Areopagite, in his account of the Divine Liturgy, which he called the 'synaxis', the gathering together, the author explains the circular movement in the following way:

> the divine sacrament of the Synaxis remains what it is, unique, simple and indivisible and yet, out of love for humanity, it is made plural in a sacred variegation of symbols. It extends itself so as to include all the hierarchical imagery. Then it draws all these various symbols together into a unity ...

> (*Ecclesiastical Hierarchy* III.3.3)

This circular movement is interpreted as going out from unity into multiplicity and returning again to unity; it is a symbol of the love of God reaching out into the created order and drawing everything back into union with Him. Put in those terms, it has a very Neoplatonic ring, echoing the fundamental triad of Neoplatonic metaphysics – rest–procession–return – a movement of expansion and contraction, diastole and systole, that undergirds all reality. It echoes, too, another circular movement: the movement of the Son from the Father and back again that recurs throughout the Fourth Gospel – 'I have come from the Father and I have come into the world; again I leave the world and go to the Father' (John 16:28) – a circular movement that issues in another circular movement – 'Just as You sent me into the world, so I send them into the world; and for their sake I sanctify myself, that they also may be sanctified in the truth' (17:18) – the movement of the disciples or apostles out into the world to draw men and women into union with God in the Church. The same circular movement underlies the Creed – 'For our sake and for our salvation he came down from heaven, and was incarnate ... crucified ... and suffered and was buried; he rose again on the third day ... and ascended into heaven'; it also underlies the Eucharist, in which we celebrate the coming forth of the Son from the Father and, in the Holy Spirit, return with the Son to the Father. It is movement, not a doctrine: a movement with its own rhythm, so that participating in, being at, the liturgy is experienced as finding oneself caught up in the rhythm of this movement of the Son to the Father.

Movement: what I want to suggest is that this sense of movement opens up an idea of presence – the presence of God – in a rather different way from what might seem to be implied by the phrase 'the practice of the presence of God'. It is not a presence that we might approach, or realize, or foster, or maintain – all senses included in the notion of *practising* the presence of God, but presence more in the sense of an encounter, a meeting.

I want to explore what I mean by this by developing two examples. The first example has to do with the way in which the Real Presence of Christ is marked in the Catholic Church (and many Anglican churches). By which I mean, reservation of the Blessed Sacrament, veneration given to the Sacrament, visiting the sacrament and praying before it, and in particular Solemn Exposition of the Host and the service of Benediction. Several converts from the Catholic west (including Anglo-Catholicism) have commented to me that it is this that, at least to begin with, they miss when becoming Orthodox (indeed, I found that myself). In Orthodox churches, although the Holy Gifts (as they are referred to) are reserved in a pyx on the holy table, there is no specific veneration of the Holy Gifts, reserved on the Holy Table: the perpetually burning light is a mark of the sanctuary, within the sanctuary the holy table itself is venerated, the gospel book, the cross, the icons … but not specifically the reserved Holy Gifts. This is true except on one liturgical occasion: the celebration of the Liturgy of the Presanctified Gifts, which takes place two or three times a week during Lent. It might seem to be some kind of parallel to, or equivalent of, the Western service of Benediction: throughout the service, the Holy Gifts are venerated, both with prostrations and with incense. It is also a deeply meditative service, a quiet service; this is noticed more, I suppose, by the celebrating priest, as, in contrast with the Divine Liturgy, he is not given lots of prayers to say silently – he censes and venerates in silence. The structure of the service is a kind of extended Vespers, with small litanies between the *staseis* of the *kathisma* of the psalter that is read as normal at vespers (each *kathisma* is divided into three *staseis*). During each of these litanies, the priest, behind the iconostasis, prepares the paten with the Holy Gifts, takes it solemnly to the table of preparation, and completes the preparation by filling the chalice with wine. Vespers continue with prayers of supplication, during which the holy table and the Holy Gifts are venerated, and then, after the readings and the usual litanies after the readings, there takes place the Great Entrance, as at a normal Liturgy, only this time it is the Holy Gifts themselves that are carried in procession, and all prostrate themselves, while the choir sings the following, instead of the Cherubic hymn:

> Now the powers of heaven worship with us invisibly. For behold, the King of glory enters. Behold the sacrifice, mystical and fully accomplished, is escorted in. With faith and love let us draw near, that we may become partakers of life eternal. Alleluia, alleluia, alleluia!

There are two things that seem to me striking about these ceremonies. First, the clear and emphatic sense of the real presence of Christ in the Holy Gifts, but moreover the sense not just of the presence of Christ, but the sense of the completion of the Eucharistic sacrifice: Christ is present, the lamb sacrificed from the beginning of the world. In the celebration of the Eucharist we join in his sacrifice; at the liturgy of the Presanctified Gifts, we are present at the Eucharistic sacrifice, 'mystical and fully accomplished'. The lack of prayers for the priest underlines this sense that there is nothing more to do: it is all done, both Christ's sacrifice on the Cross and the recalling, the re-presentation, of this in the Eucharist. Christ is present, but not just as a presence; he is present as the fully accomplished sacrifice. Secondly, the veneration of Christ in the Holy Gifts takes place liturgically – as part of the liturgical action, more precisely as the Holy Gifts move from the altar, through the body of the Church, and back to the holy table within the altar, whence they will be brought out as the Holy Gifts, offered to the Holy People of God. The real presence is celebrated, not as just there, but as the presence of One who is coming to us, coming to encounter us, and to give himself to us: Christ is the one who is coming, ὁ ἐρχόμενος – the term that is repeated throughout the liturgy, in the creed, the 'one who is coming to judge the living and the dead', in the *Sanctus, Εὐλογημένος ὁ ἐρχόμενος,* 'Blessed is he who is coming …'. And then, as in the Divine Liturgy, the Holy Gifts are brought by the deacon, or the priest, through the holy doors to the people, with the exclamation: 'With fear of God, in faith and love draw near!' Christ is the one who comes to us in the Holy Gifts, and at this point in the Liturgy we all prostrate ourselves before Christ who has come among us. In the Liturgy, we encounter Christ, as he comes to us in the Holy Gifts and we receive them in Holy Communion: this is an encounter that enables us, as we go out into the world (the true 'liturgy after the liturgy'), to encounter Christ in those we encounter, especially those in need.

So from this perspective the practice of the presence of God is not just recollection; instead, it is attention: attention to Christ as he encounters us in the Holy Gifts, attention to Christ as we encounter him in others – 'inasmuch as you have done it to one of the least of my brothers, you have done it to me'.

There are occasions when this movement in the Liturgy, with which I started, is formalized: the circular movement of censing becomes a dance, or what is called a dance. This is my second example. At the celebration of two of the sacraments – marriage and ordination – it is called the 'Dance of Isaias', so called because of the allusion to the prophet Isaias and his prophecy about Emmanuel in the verses that are sung:

> Rejoice, Isaias! The Virgin is with child, and has borne a Son, Emmanuel, both God and man; and Orient is his Name; whom we magnify and call the Virgin blessed.

> O Holy Martyrs, who have fought the good fight and have received your crowns: Pray unto the Lord that he will have mercy on our souls.

> Glory to you, Christ our God, boast of the Apostles, joy of the Martyrs, whose preaching is the consubstantial Trinity.

These are the texts at the wedding service; the same texts, in a different order, are used at ordinations. While the texts are being sung, the newly married couple, led by the priest with a censer, go around a table in the centre of the church three times. At an ordination, the dance of Isaias takes place immediately before the ordination, as the one to be ordained is led around the holy table three times. In both cases, the dance takes place anti-clockwise – widdershins. Another similar 'dance' takes place at the sacrament of baptism, in which the newly-baptized is carried (in the case of a baby) anti-clockwise round the font, led by the priest with a censer, while, 'As many as have been baptized into Christ have put on Christ, Alleluia!' is sung. All these dances – around the table or the font – complete a circular movement, that is be to seen as the beginning of an ever-expanding circle reaching out into the world, where the marriage will be lived out, in which the priesthood will be exercised and where the baptized will live his life in Christ.

In traditional Orthodox life, in a Greek village for example, these dances and other circular movements in the church match the round dance that is a feature of village life, on all sorts of occasions. In her book on the symbolic significance of the ceremonies of a Greek village, *Cosmos, Life, and Liturgy in a Greek Orthodox Village*, Juliet du Boulay, reflecting on how the round dance mirrors the circular movements in the Church's liturgy, suggests that each is taken into the other: the dance in the village relating the concerns of everyday life to the services in the Church, and the cycles in the Church – in the ceremonies and in the cycles of the day, the month, the year – giving meaning and healing to the marred nature of fallen life. She comments:

> The fallen world, then, is a living presence alongside the unfallen one; but it is felt to be possible at any time to make a reconnection with the timeless world beyond this middle ground of the cosmos and of time, and this in turn brings about a series of radical transformations.
>
> The action which is felt to reconnect with this timeless world, and to transform the doomed cycle of the fallen world, has been described again and again in the typical sayings of the villagers. It is the movement away from the evil choice towards the good, away from the devil and towards Christ, from the fallen consciousness and towards the paradisal one. This movement the Church's liturgy further defines as being from the remorseless sequence of cause and effect, sin and punishment, power and subjection, fate and suffering, which are locked together in the linear stream of this world's time, and towards the potentialities of the present moment, 'Today'. For in the eternal 'Today', the liberating energies of the risen Christ, and the intercession of the holy figures of the Church who have already been sanctified by him, can draw the powerless, the sinner, and the fated back into the divine world.[1]

'At any time', 'today': this very moment – the 'today' of the liturgical action, in which we find ourselves present, fundamentally at the Paschal mystery – the death and resurrection of Christ – but also at all the moments of sacred time that we celebrate in the course of the Christian Year.

Here the idea behind the movement is that the cycle of life in the world – the fallen world – is a kind of dance, halting, not quite in time, with all the frailties and failings of the fallen world, has the possibility of being drawn into the circular movement of the liturgy, in which we once again dance in step, in time, drawn after the dance of Christ. We find this image of the dance in the peroration of Clement of Alexandria's *Protreptikos*:

> O truly sacred mysteries! O pure light! In the blaze of the torches I have a vision of heaven and of God. I become holy by initiation. The Lord reveals the mysteries; He marks the worshipper with His seal, gives light to guide his way, and commends him, when he has believed, to the Father's care, where he is guarded for ages to come. These are the revels of my mysteries! If you want, be initiated, too, and dance with the angels around the unbegotten and imperishable and only true God, the Word of God joining with us in our hymn of praise …[2]

Both these examples – the Liturgy of the Presanctified Gifts and the place of dance in the celebration of some of the Sacraments in particular and the presence of circular movement more generally – suggest to me that the practice of the presence of God, from an Orthodox perspective, is a matter of movement, of encounter – of God with us, and us with God – rather than the sustaining or fostering of a recollected sense of presence.

I want to close with two further examples or you might say, by turning to some of the things you might have expected me to write about – icons and the Jesus Prayer. I shall treat these very briefly, as I think I have already adequately developed the principles for understanding what an Orthodox perspective on the practice of the presence of God might amount to.

Icons: they might well be regarded as a kind of presence, and the Western use of icons as a focus for meditation, often (I have noticed, especially in churches in France) alongside the Blessed Sacrament, seems to me to treat them like that. I think, however, that icons are better seen as an encounter, inviting a response, the response of deepening our relationship with Christ, the Mother of God, and the saints: a process of deepening that roots us in the fellowship of Christ, and defines who we are as we live in the world.

And, finally, the Jesus Prayer is the use of the prayer, 'Lord Jesus Christ, Son of God, have mercy on me, a sinner': especially, in the Russian tradition, the Jesus Prayer is seen as focusing on the *Name*, the Name which, when invoked, realizes a presence. But, what is involved is not so much the consciousness of a presence as the Reality of God with us, Emmanuel. There are a few points worth unfolding here. First of all, the recitation of the Jesus Prayer is the recitation of a *prayer*, an address to Jesus, an address that sums up our belief in him as our Lord, the Messiah fulfilling the hopes and longings of Israel and the whole world, the Son of God who has come to give us his 'great mercy', as so many of the liturgical verses close. It is not a mantra; it has a meaning, and that meaning sums up the whole of the Christian faith in God the Trinity, the Incarnation, and our destination in God. Furthermore, the invocation of the Name recalls the Temple tradition of the Old Testament, where the Temple, or the Tabernacle, is the place where God has chosen to place his name; it is the place where by invoking his Name, we know that we are heard, for in invoking the Name, we find ourselves in his presence.

For Sergius Bulgakov, the Name of Jesus is a wonderful gift to Christians, those who name themselves by his Name. He contrasted the invocation of the Name of Jesus with the invocation of the Name of God in the Hebrew Temple:

> The Name of Jesus is given 'at every time, at every hour' (the final prayer of the canonical hours). We should be quite conscious of this difference, of this opposition, even, between the Name of transcendent Divinity, remote and terrible, only dwelling in the Temple, according to the inflexible witness of Scripture, and the Name of Jesus, of which every heart is the temple, and every believer the priest, bearing the seal of the Name.

The recitation of the Jesus Prayer is not just the recitation of a short prayer that in some way changes our consciousness, or helps us to achieve recollection; instead, it is calling on the Name, the coming of God among us 'in grace and truth': an encounter of Christ coming to us, and our response of love and worship.

Notes

1 Juliet du Boulay, *Cosmos, Life, and Liturgy in a Greek Orthodox Village* (Limni: Harvey, 2009), p. 400.
2 Clement of Alexandria, *Protreptikos* 12. Translation modified from G. W. Butterworth in Loeb Classical Library (Cambridge, MA/London, 1919), p. 257.

7   To feel so as to understand

Hadewijch of Brabant and the legacy of St. Anselm

Rachel Smith

Introduction

In her seventh *Vision*, Hadewijch of Brabant (fl. first half of the thirteenth century) describes being overcome by a desire 'to have full fruition of my Beloved, and to understand and taste him to the full'. To have such a complete enjoyment and understanding of God means, she writes, 'to desire that his Humanity should to the fullest extent be one in fruition with my humanity'. The crucial requirement for union with God is, for Hadewijch, Christ's human nature meeting her own, an encounter in which fruition is marked, paradoxically, by 'suffering, pains and misery, and living in great new grief of soul'.[1]

The theological sources of Hadewijch's focus on the humanity of Christ with the concomitantly embodied descriptions of desire for God are typically considered to be Cistercian – Bernard of Clairvaux and William of Saint-Thierry, in particular – and the Augustinian canon, Richard of St. Victor.[2] However, as Rob Faesen and John Arblaster have recently noted, Hadewijch knew Anselm's *Cur deus homo*,[3] and she lived in a milieu profoundly affected by what Richard Southern called the 'Anselmian transformation'.[4] The elevation of Christ's human nature in Anselm's reconfiguration of the salvation narrative as a drama unfolding between God and humanity, a humanity redeemed by a saviour for whom possession of the fullness of human nature is essential to his soteriological capacities, is clearly articulated in *Cur deus homo*.[5] Christ's suffering and death for the sake of love was likewise central to Anselm's *The Prayers and Meditations* as a key site of contemplation for the penitent by means of the faculty of the imagination given redemptive capacities as the place in which Christ is made present.[6] For Hadewijch, as for Anselm, the humanity of Christ is the key – and usually ignored – means of salvation, a humanity that demands, as she is repeatedly told in her *Visions* by Christ himself, and as she exhorts readers in her *Letters*, that one who seeks redemption 'live as a human being'.

For Anselm, Christ's humanity is not only essential to his capacity to make satisfaction to the Father on behalf of all, but a central means by which the individual might resolve the problem of the gap between experience and language, between life and confession. *The Prayers and Meditations* elaborates the vicissitudes faced by the person who speaks of and to God. It repeatedly addresses a subject sunk in what it refers to as 'dullness' or 'torpor', one who does not feel, and so does not understand, the scope of his or her sin. This lack of an affective response to the speaker's existential situation is not simply a matter of an inability to perceive a personal state, but entails an inability to comprehend key theological propositions, most crucially in the devotional works, that human beings are creatures fallen into a state of sin from which they cannot rescue themselves, and therefore require a salvific act by a redeemer unmarked by sin. *The Prayers and Meditations* suggests that one must feel in order to understand; only with the affective realization of propositional content does theological argument become understood and efficacious, capable of repairing the soul's damaged likeness to God; if such an appropriation does not happen, the speaker may profess accurate statements that nevertheless have no purchase in his or her life.

The Prayers and Meditations harnesses the imagination in order to render vivid the speaker's situation in relation to God by making present the events of Christ's incarnation and the lives of his friends, the saints. In the face of God's body made vulnerable to what Anselm argued are the infinitely significant transgressions of the sinner, the *contrast* between the sinful soul and the undeserved generosity of the divine becomes apparent, a revelation of the distance between the soul and Christ that had been unrecognized. The presence of God in and through the imagination is the solution to the speaker's alienation, for that presence contains the force necessary to puncture the lassitude of a soul made dull by sin, a force derived from its intimate corporeality. Anselm thus describes meditating on the events of Christ's life and his words as a 'tasting' a 'chewing', a 'swallowing' so as to understand.[7] The puncture of conscience that arises from such meditation is what Christian tradition named the peculiar grief of compunction, a 'pain of the spirit' experienced when the soul is awakened to its sinful state. This pain causes the soul to perceive its need for divine help and thus gives rise to a desire for God.[8]

Anselm further suggests that sensible, affective knowledge of Christ (*sentio*) is possible in Eucharistic communication and through transformation of the baptized person into Christ's likeness. The resolution sought by the compunctive soul is conformity and a unitive apprehension of Christ.

Like Anselm, Hadewijch seeks an alignment of word and affect, considering how best one bears witness to the confession that God became fully human. The effect of the disorientation of the will for Hadewijch, however, is not a *lack* of feeling, but the soul's inclination to escape from the burden of human existence into an entirely pleasurable union with God. Like the Benedictine monk, Hadewijch considers this question of alignment through the principal means of Christ's humanity. With Hadewijch, thinking of Christ in his humanity is not primarily about creating a compunctive 'I' by seeing herself in contrast to the greatness of God. Rather, Christ's human life in all its abjection, suffering, and vulnerability is what one must live and become in order to 'grow up' into a redeemed and redemptive humanity. Christ is a figure with whom she radically identifies. Only through living in the forsakenness and limitation of the human condition does one come to the 'divinity' of Christ. What Anselm prays before receiving the Eucharist – that he might be 'planted in the likeness of [Christ's] death and resurrection',[9] uniting with him such that he obtains an experiential knowledge of God – Hadewijch significantly elaborates as a programme at once ethical and mystical. To speak doctrinal confession in the fullness of truth means to live the madness of love exemplified by the incarnation and recapitulated in the Eucharist, a love that pours itself out without hope of recompense. The Eucharistic table becomes for Hadewijch the whole of life, and human experiences of limitation and failure become sacramental manifestations of Christ. Hadewijch thus figures presence as bound to absence, for Christ's experiences of forsakenness in the 'exile' of his incarnation are central marks of his human life; experiences of absence may therefore become, for a believer, manifestations of divinity.

In this chapter, I will consider the Anselmian legacy in Hadewijch's works by examining the way in which each author articulates the role of Christ's humanity for spiritual progress. I am here considering only *one* suggestive site of Anselm's afterlife, suggestive insofar as it invites us to see the ways in which Anselm's attention to Christ's humanity is taken up and reconfigured in the work of a thirteenth-century, female theologian. The key Anselmian texts I will consider are *The Prayers and Meditations*, the *Proslogion*, and *Cur deus homo*. Reading Hadewijch in relation to Anselm, in turn, contextualizes some of her key teachings differently than is often the case, with the emphasis historically on the Cistercian, Victorine, and courtly sources of her thought.

'My soul, be watchful; my wretchedness, rouse yourself'[10]: Anselm and the problem of affective rectitude

To feel what one speaks might be called affective rectitude. For Anselm, rectitude (*rectitudo*) is the truth that is present when both sign and signified are properly aligned in such a way that language reflects the order of existent reality. The rectitude that is the foundation of true speech exists independently of signs; words neither give nor remove being from an object whose existence is founded upon God's action, not the human speaker's utterance.[11] God is the Truth upon which all contingent truths are based, for he is the creator of everything to which language refers, and the 'eternal truth toward which all other truths – of will, intellect, fact, word, action – are oriented'.[12] Because of this source and end of all in divine truth, love and knowledge are inseparable for Anselm.[13] If the speaker utters words that entail but do not engage the will, their utterance may have significance but not affective rectitude.

The search for affective rectitude renders impossible any understanding of Anselm's thought in isolation from his consideration of feeling. This has not, however, been the dominant mode of approach to his corpus.[14] Eileen Sweeney offers perhaps the most comprehensive attempt[15] to overcome a division between Anselm's speculative philosophy and devotional works by countering arguments that maintain a division – however complementary – between the aims of the two forms.[16] She argues that 'Anselm's corpus ... is a single project in which knowledge of self and God are inextricably linked'. The purpose of the Anselmian project in all aspects is, she writes, union with God.[17] Argument and prayer emerge from and perform Anselm's desire for the Word. In both his devotional and his speculative works, Anselm poses insoluble problems 'in order to make his way toward the perfect mirror of reality in language'.[18] Anselm aims for union with God, in Sweeney's account, by uniting word and thing.

Such union, however, requires not only the joining of word and thing, but word, thing, *and* the speaking subject, who must perform the difficult task of 'putting on' the words that accurately signify things in order to enable the reunion which God-language solicits. Although the speaker may seem to be implied by the act of using language, Anselm's works in fact demonstrate that there is often a profound lack of congruence between the words uttered by a person – even those words that are true – and the speaker's capacity to feel or experience (*sentire*) the reality to which they refer. The soul grows into understanding according to a stadial narrative in which the process of faith seeking understanding involves the growth of experiential knowledge.

'Why do I not experience what I have found?': Anselm's *Proslogion*

Anselm's *Proslogion* is a work of 'Meditation on the Meaning of Faith', as he initially considered naming it.[19] It is, then, a meditative treatise, a work of speculation in the register of prayer,[20] connected temporally as well as in content and form, to its contemporary, *The Prayers and Meditations*.[21] Although it does not contain vivid imagery depicting Christ or the saints, it emphasizes on the importance of feeling. At the centre of this work describing the fruit of the labour to find the *unum argumentum* for the existence and nature of God, Anselm pauses to note that words may be true but nevertheless remain hollow for the speaker. Anselm seeks to lift the reader, in Louis Mackey's phrase, to a more 'intimate cognition' of the divine. It is the argument's perfect union of word and thing in the context of this allocution, Mackey further maintains, that makes possible such intimate cognition.[22] The *Proslogion*, however, marks not only the significant capacities of language – its ability to signify truthfully divine reality – but also the way in which the speaker remains untouched by such truth.

In Chapter 14, at the very centre of the text,[23] he writes:

> O my soul,
> Have you found what you were looking for? I was seeking God,
> And I have found that he is above all things,
> And that than which nothing greater can be thought
> [I]f I have found him,
> Why do I not experience what I have found?
> Lord God,
> If my soul has found you,
> Why has it no experience of you?[24]

After a long struggle, Anselm finds the 'faithful definition of the Word'[25] as 'that than which nothing greater can be thought'. In this verbal formula, Anselm achieves rightness of theological speech, that rectitude (*rectitudo*) in which the sign accurately reflects the object signified. The phrase 'certifies its own reference', Mackey writes, for the proof requires 'no other proof than itself'.[26] Thus, the '(misleadingly) so-called ontological proof of God's existence is more aptly described a proof of the ontological reliability of language', for it 'locate[s] the moment of linguistic soundness, the plenitude of presence from which other language may deviate but to which it is always bound'.[27]

After recollecting his discovery of the proof that came to him after his prayer that he understands the one in whom 'we believe',[28] Anselm asserts the persistent difficulty in which theological work and spiritual life unfolds: the impossibility of language to arrive at or capture divine reality, and thus for the human being to experience the referent towards which language presses. Having traversed the ontological gap by means of a language grounded in the Word, the gap now reasserts itself within the speaker. Faithfully confessing the Word and thereby finding what was sought, he or she yet does not 'experience' (*sentit*) that Word. Despite the plenitude of presence within the verbal formula that allows him to say he has 'found' what he sought, not all that can be sought can be found. The narrator speaks with rectitude, but remains outside of the fullness of that speech, unable to 'feel' its meaning.

The experience of God as absent may be a result of two different things and thus its significance can radically diverge.[29] Its first cause is the sheer contrast between human and divine natures, the former finite, contingent, and bodily while the latter is infinite, non-contingent, and incorporeal. Anselm writes that in striving for greater vision he sees only darkness,

> or rather I do not see darkness
> which is no part of you,
> but I see that I cannot see further
> because of my own darkness ...
> The truth is I am darkened by myself
> and also dazzled by you.
> I am clouded by my own smallness
> and overwhelmed by your immensity;
> I am restricted by my own narrowness
> and mastered by your wideness.[30]

God is, he thus reflects in Chapter 15, going further than the original formula of Chapter 2, 'something greater than it is possible to think about'. The asymmetry between divine and human renders mortal faculties incapable of experiencing and therefore understanding God. The senses are too limited to pin down the immensity of God:

> But whatever I see, I see through it,
> like a weak eye
> that sees what it does by the light of the sun,
> though it cannot look at the sun itself.
> My understanding cannot take it in,
> it is too bright, I cannot receive it.[31]

The asymmetry that leads to a failure of perception in this case incites the seeker's desire: 'Tell me what you are, beyond what I have seen,/ so that I may see clearly what I desire.'[32] The very impossibility of its aspiration is salutary, driving the one who prays further in the spiritual itinerary.

A second, very different, reason for the failure to experience that which has been found is not natural for creaturely life, but is sin, punished by God with pain, including the pain of the disorder of the will.[33] Although slippage between the two causes can easily occur, the moral cause of disjunction between knowledge and experience has a fundamentally different source and effect than the distinction between creature and creator. In the moral case, the senses are not only of a different order from God's, but 'have been hardened (*obriguerunt*), dulled (*obstupuerunt*), and blocked (*obstructi*) by the ancient sickness of sin'.[34]

The dullness of the soul's senses leading to a lack of awareness or understanding is a key problem addressed by *The Prayers and Meditations*. This dullness not only obscures the individual's capacity to see God, but the moral state that is the source of such faulty perception; sin blocks the capacity to understand God, but more problematically, the capacity to appreciate one's own sinfulness, to be 'stirred up' by its presence, which would, Anselm writes, 'turn my lukewarmness into a fervent love of you'.[35]

'I am scarcely aware of my sins': Compunction, contrast and the imagination in *The Prayers and Meditations*.

Written in the same rhymed prose as the *Proslogion*, *The Prayers and Meditations* (and letters that accompany them) are the earliest of Anselm's works to have survived, mostly composed between 1063 and 1078 while he was prior at the Norman Abbey of Notre Dame de Bec.[36] Addressed to Christ and to particular saints, they seek to 'stir up the mind' (*excita mentem*) to love or fear of God and to undertake an interior journey that issues in compunction. Anselm tells recipients – including Countess Mathilda of Tuscany and Princess Adelaide, as well as monastic friends – to read these works 'not cursorily or quickly, but slowly and with profound and deliberate meditation'.[37] The prose demands a deliberate response, for it is intricately wrought and saturated with intense feeling evoked through vivid depictions of the saints and the petitioner's state. Because of the ways in which Anselm reconfigured the ancient form of meditative prayer, rendering it more elaborate and personal, less tied to the Psalms, and filling it with 'effusive self-disclosure', and because his audience was not only male monastics, but also laywomen who read these texts privately, outside a liturgical context, Anselm has been credited with giving voice to new currents in eleventh-century spirituality and, through his innovative writing, inspiring a 'transformation' of medieval, devotional writing and practice.[38] Along with his formulation of a profoundly influential new theory of the atonement, *The Prayers and Meditations* – which were extremely popular throughout the Middle Ages[39] – are generally considered to be crucial to the rise of 'affective piety', a style of devotion notable for the cultivation of a fervent love for the humanity of Christ, compassion for his sufferings at the crucifixion, identification with Mary's grief, and an eager longing for union with God.[40]

In the first *Prayer to Mary,* Anselm writes, 'Good Lady/ a huge dullness (*stuporis*) is between you and me,/ so that I am scarcely aware of the extent of my sickness'.[41] Addressing his sins, he accuses them of having 'made my senses unfeeling with your torpor'. As in the *Proslogion*, there is an inability to feel or experience (*sensum*) a theological fact that the narrator knows, in this case, his sinfulness. The fundamental difference between the lack of feeling described in the fourteenth chapter of the *Proslogion* and this prayer, however, is that in the latter case, the narrator does not feel the enormity of his destitution because he does not register the contrast between his sickness and Mary's virtue. The prayer diagnoses the two related problems faced by the sin-sick soul: alienation and torpor. The narrator's lack of awareness gives rise to and is a result of estrangement from the saint. In the *Proslogion*, ch. 14 the narrator's inability to experience the God whom he has defined places him in a vivid space of contrasts, leading to the antitheses of his smallness, narrowness, darkness and divine immensity, and luminosity, distinctions that parallel the division between his discovery of the verbal formula and the disappointment he registers. This vision of contrast is ultimately productive, arousing the mind to intensify its inquiry. The dazzling darkness the narrator further describes in Chapter 16 not only registers a theological aporia, but depicts a vivid scene of the dynamic between the God who dwells in 'inaccessible light' and the human who nevertheless passionately pursues perception, 'crushed', 'dazzled', 'confounded', and 'mastered' by a God who is 'entirely present', 'within and around' the speaker, and yet he of whom he has 'no experience'.[42]

The *Prayer to Mary*, on the other hand, demonstrates the failure of imagination. Distance here is not productive, yielding desire for that which eludes it, but a function of alienation. The inability of the mind to rouse itself to an awareness of the sin it holds itself to have makes it unable to register the sinner's state or the saint's magnificence. Moreover, it leads to a different kind of aphasia, in this case the inability to pray.[43] Similarly, in the *Prayer to Peter,* Anselm laments that although '[a]gain and again I try to stir up my dull mind … it cannot break through the darkness of the torpor which the stains of sin have brought upon it', turning him into a 'wretched being who can neither express tribulation in words, nor find sorrow in his mind'.[44]

The Prayers and Meditations depicts, then, an impossible problem. Sin creates a 'dullness' where there should be a desire, a numbness that does not allow

Anselm to find that which exists, namely the 'sorrow in his mind'. Sin hides its tracks by occluding the eyes and hardening the heart so that its extent – in a perverse mirror of divine infinity – can neither be experienced nor named. The torpor of mind is an anaesthetized state in which pain is not recognized as such and so the desire to escape is not enflamed. In a vicious circularity, desire for God is the solution to the problem even as its lack is the problem:

> My soul wants [St. Nicholas] to turn towards God and to you,
> and it is weighed down by a heavy weight.
> It desires to direct its gaze towards you,
> and it is weighed down in a curve by a heavy weight …
> it is obscured by dark shadows.
> It makes efforts to release itself,
> but it is held in bonds of iron.[45]

These bonds are the love for earthly things, which thwart desire for God, bending love's trajectory back towards itself. He wants to turn towards the divine, but does not, in fact, want to.[46] This desire, however, is necessary to make the saint present:

> Certainly if my heart (*cor*) was contrite,
> if my heart (*viscera*) was moved within me,
> if my soul was turned to water,
> if rivers of tears flowed from my eyes,
> then I might hope that Nicholas would hear my prayers.
> Therefore, my lord, St Nicholas, stir up my spirit,
> excite my heart,
> move my mind to love according to my need,
> so that I may feel the effect of your compassion …[47]

The impossibility of disrupting this vicious circle of desirelessness and aliena- tion from God, in which the soul struggles to desire the desire that will be its cure, is structurally recapitulated in *Cur deus homo*. Here, Anselm argues that sin is an infinite debt incurred by finite human beings who are unable to make restitution and therefore cannot save themselves.[48] In the treatise, the solu- tion is the God-man, a gracious act uniting divine mercy and justice in which the divinity as a sinless human being renders the infinite satisfaction required to remove original sin.[49] In *The Prayers and Meditations*, it is Christ and the saints, by virtue of their perfect participation in Christ, who must graciously 'stir up' the spirit and 'excite [the] heart' so that the sinner's 'need and love' are commensurate.

The sinner's capacity to ask for what she does not understand or fully desire is predicated, then, on the grace that has already been given in the incarnation. It is this grace that enables desire to desire. *The Prayers and Meditations* offer skills for putting on that grace. They contain scripts that enable the reader to realize those doctrines that point to truths human and divine.[50]

The rhetoric of the prayers works in many ways to reorient the will.[51] The situation of address is one notable strategy. The *Prayers* apostrophize the saints, reciting their qualities so that their image can be vividly seen, throwing the speaker's contrasting image into relief through a verbal chiaroscuro that emerges in the speaker's search for dialogue. The *Prayers* likewise address sin, bringing it to a degree of animation that pushes back against the torpor that Anselm has diagnosed as his crucial problem. Anselm also addresses himself, listing his sins in detail, teaching him to 'be terribly afraid of' himself.[52] The vivid construction of his forlorn state described alongside the grandeur of his divine intercessors creates a landscape of contrasts that is, paradoxically, in the service of presence. Insofar as he becomes aware of his enslavement to sin and his distance from God, the greater his understanding of his need for and the meaning of the gracious response already offered by God: ascent embedded in his abasement.

The search for presence is a hallmark of affective devotion. For our purpose it is crucial to note Anselm's ability to identify deeply with the historical events of Christ's earthly life as described in the *Prayer to Christ*:

> So, as much as I can, though not as much as I ought,
> I am mindful of your passion,
> Your buffeting, your scourging, your cross, your wounds,
> How you were slain for me,
> How prepared for burial and buried ...
> Alas for me, that I was not able to see
> The Lord of Angels humbled to converse with men,
> When God, the one insulted,
> Willed to die that the sinner might live ...
> Why, O my soul, were you not there
> To be pierced by a sword of bitter sorrow
> When you could not bear
> The piercing of the side of your Saviour with a lance?
> Why could you not see with horror
> The blood that poured out of the side of your Redeemer?
> Why were you not drunk with bitter tears
> When they gave him bitter gall to drink?
> Why did you not share
> The sufferings of the most pure virgin ...?[53]

The means of communion with Christ is a turning to the imagination in order to recreate and elaborate upon the events of Christ's life. Anselm details the tears that 'drenched [Mary's] matchless face', the butchery of Christ's flesh, imagines himself with Joseph taking Christ down from the cross and mourning at the tomb, kissing the wounds on his dead body, hearing of the resurrection along with the women. The re-presencing of the lost body of the ascended Christ counters the torpor of sin, the dullness that is an absence of awareness of God. It is a work of memory that attempts to 'turn ... lukewarmness into a fervent love of you' by 'remembering and meditating on the good things you have done'.[54] If dullness is a failure of imagination, the imagination here is its cure. Should he have been present to witness Christ's passion, affect and understanding would have been joined, for he would have known the truth of the Passion by 'sharing' in the suffering of the exemplary mourner, Mary, his soul 'pierced by the sorrow' of his death. The vividness of the prayerful remembrance of the incarnation compensates for historical absence by recreating it in detail, allowing the reader to participate in its events and become an actor in its drama.

The events of Christ's life are the incarnational foundations of doctrinal propositions. In the *Meditation on Human Redemption*, the meditative counterpart to the treatise *Cur deus homo*, Anselm unfolds the wider theological narrative implied by the incarnation, and then appropriates these doctrines on an individual level. He first addresses the 'Christian soul, brought to life again out of the heaviness of death, redeemed and set free from wretched servitude by the blood of God', detailing the soteriological and Christological meaning of the passion. He then exhorts this soul, 'Rouse yourself and remember that you are risen, realize that you have been redeemed and set free.' In order to understand the meaning of the soteriological claims of faith, the meditator must 'shake off ... lethargy'.[55]

The work of memory enables intimate, embodied presence. Anselm writes that meditating on the gospel accounts is an eating of the divine:

> Taste the goodness of your Redeemer, be on fire with love for your Saviour. Chew the honeycomb of his words, suck their flavour which is sweeter than sap, swallow their wholesome sweetness. Chew by thinking, suck by understanding, swallow by loving and rejoicing.[56]

Meditation on the life of Christ and on the works that he has done for the individual who takes up this contemplation is rooted in the monastic tradition of *lectio divina*, in which the words of scripture were repeatedly read, sung, spoken, until they were assimilated to the reader, such that the reader becomes, in Abba Isaac's words to Cassian and Germanus, 'the author' of the text, one's dispositions (*affectus*) reformed in the image of the biblical script.[57] In this *Meditation*, understanding arises from tasting, chewing, swallowing the memories of Christ's life until love is incited. Only through the rhythm of meditation and prayer does one 'realize' the facts of Christ's soteriological action and its intimate implications for ourselves.

Anselm's language of tasting suggests Ps. 33:9 (*gustate et videte quoniam suavis est Deus*), a verse that was commonly used in concert with the ancient Latin wordplay on the verb *sapere*, meaning both to taste and to know, and *sapientia*, that transforming wisdom that arises from intimate communion with God, including that contact that comes from meditative reading of scripture.[58] Surprisingly Anselm does not exploit this pun in his works.[59] He does, however, have frequent recourse to the language of 'sweetness' (*suavis, dulcis*) in *The Prayers and Meditations*.[60] He thereby alludes to both Psalm 33:9 and 1 Peter 2:3 as well as the complex tradition of the spiritual senses, in which the bodily sensorium is a means for describing and understanding human knowledge of God, enabling theologians to explain how knowledge of immaterial, divine things is attained by an embodied knower.[61] As Ella Johnson notes, the theological stakes for writers who employ the language of *sapere/sapientia* (and related terms like sweetness and swallowing), is the notion that through the sense of taste humans make physical contact with God.[62] Such tasting occurs literally in the Eucharist, but also, as the metaphors of eating that proliferate in reflections on *lectio divina* imply, in the practice of meditative reading.

To eat the text, to consume the word, the language suggests, is a sacramental act. In the 'Prayer Before Receiving the Body and Blood of Christ', Anselm writes that sacramental participation, in which the elements make present the body and blood, heals the disjunction between experience and knowledge that the 'Prayer to Mary (I)' laments:

> Make me, O Lord, so to perceive with lips and heart
> And know by faith and by love,
> That by virtue of this sacrament I may deserve to be
> Planted in the likeness of your death and resurrection,
> By mortifying the old man,
> And by renewal of the life of righteousness.
> May I be worthy to be incorporated into your body
> which is the church.[63]

Through incorporation into the body of Christ, a process that refashions the subject according to the likeness of Christ's passion, the communicant is able to know in affective, intellectual, and bodily modes of knowledge. No longer is the subject split between an understanding that assents to a proposition yet leaves to one side the knowledge of feeling and sensation. Instead, the speaking subject is aware of his or her state and Christ's, both of which are *res* signified by theological speech that now possesses complete rectitude. Moreover, the 'Meditation' suggests that in some sense an experiential knowledge of God is possible through Eucharistic communion and transformation of the person into the likeness of Christ. The 'Meditation', with its Christological focus, suggests a very different possibility from what the *Proslogion* outlines: the soul that is rooted in and has 'found' God may not experience God because of the distance between humanity and divinity.

Hadewijch of Brabant and the Anselmian legacy

Hadewijch's life unfolded in a radically different context from Anselm's. We have no biographical information about her, but it seems rather certain that she lived in the first half of the thirteenth century in the Duchy of Brabant.[64]

It has been conjectured, on the basis of her writings, that her works were composed as pedagogical tools for young Beguines and often used by them paraliturgically.[65] She wrote not in the Latin of the educated (although she did read Latin), but in Middle Dutch. Her literary and theological inspirations included scripture, Augustinian and Cistercian theologians,[66] but also the songs of the troubadours, whose secular courtly love lyrics she adapted to her own theological purposes.[67]

Jozef van Mierlo, editor of her *Letters*, argues that her sixth Letter distils the key elements her teaching[68] – Hadewijch instructs her readers about what it means to love in a way that reflects being 'crucified with Christ' (Gal. 2:19) in such a way that one dies and rises again with him (Col. 3:1), who is Love (*minne*) itself.[69] The *Letters* allude to *Cur deus homo*. The Son of God, she writes, 'took the lead', modelling true virtue by doing the 'will of the Father in all things and at all times'. With

> his whole heart and his whole soul and with all his strength, in each and every circumstance, he was ready to perfect what was wanting on our part. And thus he uplifted us and drew us up by his divine power and his human justice to our first dignity, and to our liberty, in which we were created and loved, and to which we are now called …[70]

Christ, by virtue of the perfect union of the human and divine natures, compensates for the absence of power and righteousness in postlapsarian humanity who is unable to heal the damage it suffers on account of sin. The vocation of love that Christ embodies in this work of making satisfaction, paying humanity's infinite debt to the father, was paid – and this is crucial for both Anselm and Hadewijch – as a human subject to the same adversity as all humans (except that caused by sin). 'We do not find it written anywhere', she insists, 'that Christ ever, in his entire life, had recourse to his Father or his omnipotent Nature to obtain joy and repose'.[71] Christ truly and fully lived the human condition, not only while preaching, consoling, and working miracles, but particularly in his experiences of pain, shame, and distress 'even to the passion', which in another Anselmian echo, is the 'consummat[ion of] his work' of paying 'by the service of perfect fidelity, the debt of human nature to the Father's divine truth. Then *mercy and truth met together, and justice and peace kissed each other*' (Ps. 84:11).[72] Both Anselm and Hadewijch argue that in Christ the demands of divine justice – which requires that violations of God's honour be satisfied through a restorative payment made by the transgressor, and divine mercy, which desires to return humanity to its original blessedness – are reconciled.

In the first *Vision*, Christ gives an account of his experience on earth:

> [R]ecognize [that] … my body suffered sore pain, and that my hands worked faithfully, and that my new will overflowed with charity … through the whole world, upon strangers and upon friends, and that my senses languished, and that my Heart desired, and that my soul loved.[73]

Later, Christ continues the narration of his life and connects his experience to Hadewijch's own:

> And when I had worked miracles and became better known, few friends remained to me in the world. Yes, at my death almost all [those] alive abandoned me. Therefore do not let it grieve you that all persons will forsake you on account of perfect Love and because you are living in my will ...[74]

Hadewijch's experience of forsakenness (Columba Hart hypothesizes her expulsion from a community of Beguines, perhaps under threat of charges of Quietism),[75] enables her to identify with Christ, her embodiment of his abandonment by his friends while he faced persecution and murder. The salvific work of Christ's suffering – not only his death – thus continues; it manifests in the lives of those who love God.[76]

In loving fully despite such love remaining unrequited, Christ's love is excessive, functioning beyond an economy of exchange. It is this love, a love that does not seek reciprocity but loves for the sake of love itself, to which humanity is called. Such imitation is not, however, the norm; 'today', Hadewijch writes, '[w]e do not live with Christ as he lived, neither do we forsake all as Christ did, nor are we forsaken by all as Christ was'.[77] Instead, humanity is subject to the most 'pernicious evil', namely the desire to obtain evidence for the other's love, seeking proof of fidelity and reciprocity. This may be from friends or from God himself, whom

> we demand ... as a reward for our good works' by wishing 'to feel him present in this life, on the supposition that we have truly merited this and consequently that he, in his turn, should rightly do what we want him to ... we never resign ourselves to being left without recompense.[78]

A true lover of God, however, seeks to act without self-will or thought of reward, and 'without sparing, lose all for all; and learn uniquely and intrepidly the perfect life of Love'.[79] Perfect love is to live 'the one for the other'.[80] This is Trinitarian love, in which the Father and Son give themselves wholly to one another and are thereby united in the Spirit. Living for the other, willing the will of the Father, is what Christ manifests in his human life.

The requirement to live as a human being, subject to limitations and suffering, is one that most attempt to avoid. Instead, Hadewijch argues that the spiritual state to which the majority aspire is an experience of 'sweetness' in the divine presence. It is, she writes, 'supposed that people' who feel such sweetness are particularly gifted 'when in reality they suffer deep privation of God'.[81] God consoles the weak with moments of enjoyment, but often these souls are 'gentle and fruitful' only as long as the pleasure of presence persists; if it disappears, they mirror their circumstance, becoming hard, for they are not 'rooted' in the divine power that is the source of human virtue, practising 'fidelity' to the will of the other that does not 'think of the reward'.[82]

In *Letter* Six, Hadewijch describes the greed for sweetness as a desire for a fruition (*ghebruken*) that occurs in a union with the divinity that bypasses the humanity:

> Nowadays this is the way everyone loves [themselves]; people wish to live with God in consolations and repose, in wealth and power, and to share the fruition of his glory. We all indeed wish to be God with God, but God knows there are few of us who want to live as [human beings] with his Humanity, or want to carry his cross with him, or want to hang on the cross with him and pay humanity's debt to the full.[83]

To seek only the pleasure of union with God is to pursue reward and thus to be enmeshed in a logic of exchange that renders impossible the madness of Christ's love. Love of neighbour is reduced to self-love. To live one's humanity in union with Christ's is, by contrast, an act of re-presencing his life; it is the fidelity of a person to a love that seeks no recompense but performs the divine will for its own sake. Living one's human life as Christ did, subjected to mortal limitation yet loving without measure, is the solution to the disorientation of the will that seeks its own pleasure and so cannot love that which it confesses to love. Through such union with Christ's humanity mature union with the God is attained:

> With the Humanity of God you must live here on earth, in the labors and sorrow of exile, while within your soul you love and rejoice with the omnipotent and eternal Divinity in sweet abandonment. For the truth of both is one single fruition. And just as Christ's Humanity surrendered itself on earth to the will of the Majesty, you must here with Love surrender yourself to both in unity. Serve humbly under their sole power ...[84]

Union with the humanity of Christ, in service and exile for the sake of love, is necessary for uniting with Christ's divinity and thus for participating in Trinitarian love. Christ's humanity is the means through which union with divinity is possible, for 'the truth of both is one single fruition'. Here Hadewijch articulates a spiritual dynamic founded on the Chalcedonian principle of the hypostatic union, in which the two natures of Christ are perfectly one and yet remain without confusion; the fruition experienced living the humanity (*ghebreken*), in which one suffers and fails, and the divinity (*ghebruken*), in which one experiences blissful enjoyment – as different each may seem at a phenomenological level – is one. Both are found, 'in living in the will of the Other'.[85] The person who seeks union abandons their own will in perfect obedience to the demands of love in imitation of the human Christ's obedience to the father.

The suffering of Christ, made present by the devout person, is not functioning here primarily, then, as a way of contrasting the soul and God in order to stir up compunction, but as a richly imagined site of identification in which the Christian continues the work of Christ and thereby 'become[s] what [she is], and … grasp[s] what [she has]'.[86] Thus in the first *Vision*, Christ tells Hadewijch to 'never fail anyone until the day when I say to you: 'Your work is totally accomplished' (cf. John 19:30)!'.[87] Christ promises to speak the same words to Hadewijch, should she persist in her life of love, that he spoke at the conclusion of his own life. In *Letter* Seventeen, Hadewijch describes her transformation into the body of Christ not as promise, but as a memory. She writes of a Eucharistic vision she had on the feast of the Ascension. At the moment of consecration when 'his Son came upon the altar', she received a kiss from Christ. This union, signified by the kiss, in turn enabled her to come into the presence of the Father:

> Having been made one with him, I came before his Father. There the Father took the Son to himself with me and took me to himself with the Son. And in this Unity into which I was taken and where I was enlightened, I understood this Essence and knew it more clearly than, by speech, reason or sight, one can know anything that is knowable on earth.[88]

The Father here 'took Him [the Son] for me, and me for Him' (*daer nam hi hem over mi ende mi over hem*). The life of the person who lives *minne* as Christ did, without reserve or calculation, becomes a sacrament, making present the deity in humanity such that distinctions between self and other, human and divine, are overcome. In this state of union, Paul Mommaers writes, meditation upon the life of Christ (such as Anselm undertakes in *The Prayers and Meditations*) is possible and licit but no longer necessary.[89]

Divine union is given a clear Eucharistic expression in the seventh *Vision*. Placed in the centre of her *Book of Visions*, Hadewijch writes that on Pentecost Sunday at Matins – the feast that commemorates the pouring out of the Holy Spirit on the disciples and the Virgin Mary so that they might become participants in Trinitarian life[90] – she was overcome with a desire 'to have full fruition (*ghebrukene*) of my Beloved, and to understand and taste him to the full. I desired that his Humanity should to the fullest extent be one in fruition with my humanity …' and, through this union with the humanity, enter into the perfection of 'grow[ing] up in order to be God with God, by giving 'satisfaction' to God 'in all great sufferings'.[91] Christ then comes forth from the altar, as a beautiful young man, and gives himself to Hadewijch 'in the shape of the sacrament', whereupon

> he came himself to me, took me entirely in his arms, and pressed me to him; and all my members felt his in full felicity (*in alle hare ghenoeghen* – as to their satisfaction), in accordance with the desire of my heart and my humanity … Also then, for a short while, I had the strength to bear this; but soon, after a short time, I lost that manly beauty outwardly in the sight of his form. I saw him completely come to nought and so fade and all at once dissolve that I could no longer recognize or perceive him outside me, and I could no longer distinguish him within me. Then it was to me as if

we were one without difference. It was thus: outwardly, to see, taste, and feel as one can outwardly taste, see, and feel in the reception of the outward Sacrament. So can the Beloved, with the loved one, each wholly receive the other in all full satisfaction *ghenoech* of the sight, the hearing, and the passing away of the one in the other.

After that I remained in a passing away in my Beloved, so that I wholly melted away in him and nothing any longer remained to me of myself ...[92]

The assimilation into Christ's life through the practice of the virtues of love, living Christ's humanity, occurs here in a sacramental register in which Hadewijch 'loses herself' to Christ, becoming 'one without difference', eating his body and being received by him.[93] In this mutual reception, she finds fulfilled the desire to 'satisfy' God that opened the vision.

What this satisfaction consists in has been a source of contention among scholars. I would argue that the term 'satisfaction' (*ghenoech*), central to and recurring in the *Vision*, can be properly accounted for only in light of Hadewijch's notion of the role of Christ's humanity in union with God. Typically, 'satisfaction' has been understood in the register of pleasure. Thus the statement that 'my members felt his in full felicity' (*in alle hare ghenoeghen*) is often read as a description of an enjoyable physical encounter with Christ's body that then passes over into the bliss of union. However, as Rob Faesen notes, the 'basic theme [of the *Vision*] concerns ... how the *human* might participate in the life of *God* – which is a life of absolute love'.[94] As earlier established, such participation is possible only through union with Christ in his humanity, who loved with absolute love marked inevitably by suffering and death. Thus Faesen argues that Christ allows Hadewijch to feel his humanity – his suffering in its absolute fullness – for as long as she could bear it, in her flesh.[95]

To understand the meaning of 'satisfaction' in this way, as satisfying God by living love as did the *human* Christ, a love that leads to the death of will and body, draws Hadewijch's thought and lexicon again into Anselm's view of salvation in Christ. Literally meaning to be 'enough' for God, by indicating that her initial desire to give 'satisfaction in all great sufferings' in a life of suffering love and Eucharistic consumption was fulfilled, Hadewijch suggests that in the wake of the incarnation, a person united to Christ becomes capable of the very thing that Anselm contends had been impossible for human beings to do, namely 'satisfy' God. It was this impossibility that necessitated the singular advent of the God-man who, as a human being, suffered and died to pay the debt that humans had incurred.[96] For Anselm as for Hadewijch, satisfaction is impossible apart from the humanity of Christ, but for Hadewijch the human being redeemed through the God-man performs again the work of satisfaction.

However, I would argue that there is also a kind of pleasure here, one that is no less Christological. The 'full satisfaction' of union 'without difference' found in Eucharistic consumption entails the perfect symmetry of the senses and their object, such that the 'seeing', 'tasting', and 'feeling' perfectly perceive and pass away into the other, overcoming that painful gap described in the *Proslogion*, in which the human sensorium is unable to apprehend God. The passage is highly reminiscent of Anselm's *Meditation on Human Redemption*, in which outward reception of the sacrament enables conformity to Christ and an embodied apprehension of the divine. The sensory experience of the 'outward form' of the sacrament here gives way, however, by virtue of perfect union, to the negation of form and experience. In assimilating Christ, Hadewijch loses herself and the 'beauty of his form', leaving her unable to perceive him within or without her. At this point she 'wholly melted away in him and nothing any longer remained to me of myself'. Such 'passing away' is a description of the 'highest love', of being transfused into the will of another.

Given the Christological nature of this union, however, melting into God cannot be understood as a final state of insulating pleasure. By grounding the desolation, suffering, and failure of Christ's human life, in her refusal to recuperate this pain by gathering it, without remainder, into an experience of divine bliss, but maintaining the necessity of its presence within what Paul Mommaers calls the dynamic of the 'being-one', Hadewijch unites two contraries, exile and union, forsakenness and inherence.[97] To imagine union as a transcendence of human limitation, a surpassing of Christ's humanity by means of consuming his body, would be to retreat to the very fantasy she critiques in *Letter* Six and it would not be to live love in its fullness. The final and 'highest' name given to love in *Poem in Couplets* 16, is 'Hell', for 'In Love nothing else is acquired/ But disquiet and torture without pity; Forever to be in unrest,/ Forever assault and new persecution …'[98]

The lover secures torment because love is an abyss, 'unfathomable'. The abyssal nature of love calls forth an answering abyss of the soul:

> But they who stand ready to content Love are also eternal and unfathomable. For their *conversation is in heaven* (Phil. 3:20), and their souls follow everywhere their Beloved (Apoc. 14:4), who is unfathomable. But then, although they are loved with an eternal love (Jer. 31:3), they also are never attained by the depths of Love, so that they can never attain the one they love or content him; and nevertheless they will nothing else – either to content God or to die in the attempt – nothing else matters.[99]

The attempt of the soul to 'content' the infinite leads to the continuous pouring out of the soul in a desire that does not cease, rendering the soul, as love, an unfathomable abyss, bottomless in its response. The highest interior expression of such an uncalculated love is what Hadewijch calls 'noble unfaith', the renunciation of the belief that love will be requited while maintaining the belief that 'all the love is on our side'.[100] Unfaith, she writes, is 'higher than any fidelity that is not abysmal', namely any fidelity that is content to possess a limited quantity of love, and to rest in a sense of assurance – *fiducia* – that the soul's love is satisfactory. In other words, a soul has unfaith insofar as it becomes conformed to God and thus loves in an abyssal manner.[101] The soul that gives and finds satisfaction in perfect union is simultaneously the soul that remains 'forever in unrest'.

Paul Mommaers argues that the dynamic of the human experience of love arises from the soul's awareness of its union with the deity, on the one hand, and on the other, its consciousness of an inability to satisfy its debt to love, both because it cannot attain infinite proportions, and because it often feels abandoned and forsaken by human and divine others. This incapacity to satisfy is experienced by the soul as a lack, a failure (*ghebreken*).[102] And yet, because of the adoption of human limitation and failure by Christ, this very failure comes not to be a sign of the soul's unworthiness, but its conformity to Christ who took up limitation and failure and in so doing, transfigured it.[103] Through this transformation of the significance of limitation, desire – the sign of lack – is simultaneously a mark of fulfilment. God as abyss remains uncaptured. And yet this abyss calls forth the soul's desire in such a way that Hadewijch speaks of the mutual abysses (*afgront*) of the soul and God.[104] The union between lack and fulfilment is the condition of the possibility for a spiritual progress that is endless.[105]

Hadewijch conceives of this dynamism of loving union between presence and absence Christologically, modelled on the paradox of Christ's life: utterly forsaken, abandoned, emptied of divinity he is yet perfectly, indissolubly, united with, and giving fullest expression to the *minne* that is God. The absence of divinity at the heart of the mystery of redemption means that absence is folded into fruition. The notion of presence and union are, therefore, transformed or, Hadewijch writes, 'enlarged'.[106] She enjoins readers to renounce the desire for a presence conceived solely as the sweetness of merging, and to seek instead to unite with the humanity whose failure, desolation, and abandonment is the condition for the saving desire of the abyssal soul. God who is wholly other, unfathomable and is yet utterly present, consumed by and united with the soul.

Conclusion

With Anselm we saw the turn to the humanity of Christ in *The Prayers and Meditations* as a solution to the problem of an affective alienation in language, the gap between experience and knowledge, articulated in the *Proslogion* and *The Prayers and Meditations*. These devotional and meditative works harness the imagination, seeking to make present the God who has already ascended. Presence through the imaginative rendering of the historical events of Christ's crucifixion enables the speaker to witness Christ's torture and, in the face of its graphic reality, to feel the contrast between its own listlessness and the passion and perfection of the God-man. This awakening through dissimilarity made visible, stings the soul into a state of compunction, whereby the speaker realizes the scope of his or her sin, arousing a desire for God and gratitude for what has been done to heal the soul. To feel one's sin and therefore one's need for God is to have an affect congruent with the confession of faith; it is to attain affective rectitude. Only through such feeling is understanding found, an understanding in which the gap between experience and language is closed.

Like Anselm, Hadewijch seeks to enliven desire. The problem she addresses is not, however, a dullness of feeling but the orientation of affect entirely towards union with God, a desire conceived solely as the gratifying presence of divinity. As with Anselm, attention to and making present Christ's humanity is the solution to the disordered will. Hadewijch's Christ is not represented primarily as a vividly rendered image of pain in order to contrast his virtue with the soul's sin (although there is a powerfully exhortative element in her pedagogical works, a lament that we are not living up to 'who we are'). Rather, the accent falls on identification. Christ's broken humanity is a sign of the divine act of union with the limitations of human life such that these very limits and the failures become vehicles of divine union. For Hadewijch limitation, perceived absence, and human failure, are likewise present in Christ's life. If properly understood, our experience of such trials is nothing other than Christomimetic; loving in and from this human context is the way in which Christ is made present again and again in the deeds and feelings of his lovers.

For Anselm, too, compunctive desire moves towards union with Christ through a taking on of his death and resurrection in life and in the Eucharist. Hadewijch radicalizes this claim, both by elaborating an ethical programme that encompasses the entirety of a life in the world and with her daring treatments of union. The perfect presence she describes, however, is incited, like the desire detailed by Anselm in the *Proslogion* by the soul's inability to fully possess or satisfy the Beloved.[107]

For neither Hadewijch nor Anselm is theology an activity of pure, disembodied intellect. Rather, it is a profoundly affective questioning that emerges from our embodied state, with all the limitations that attend. Such questioning is answered by a likewise embodied divinity and is inseparable from our way of life. To speak of and to God requires a transformation of affect and ethics if it is to be true. For Anselm, theological speech must transform and be congruent with the speaker's desire. This is made possible through the strategic use of imagination, narrative, and participation in sacramental life. For Hadewijch, one must 'live Christ' by loving for love's sake, without seeking recompense. For both figures, only through an embodied, intimate presence with a God both human and divine, is true insight attained. As Hadewijch writes in her fourteenth *Vision*,

> For each revelation I had seen partly according to what I was myself, and partly according to my having been chosen; but now I saw this ... to which I was chosen in order that I might taste Man and God in one knowledge, what no man could do unless he were as God, and wholly such as he was who is our Love.[108]

For both Anselm and Hadewijch theology is much more than discourse about God. Theology is a response to God. Theology is not a theorizing that stands at a distance from God, but a relationship that transforms desire and provides the very possibilities of theology. One cannot understand, writes Hadewijch, unless one is 'as he who is our Love', unless one is the love that is the Beloved or, as Anselm puts it, unless one is 'planted in the likeness of Christ's death and resurrection'. For each theologian, their 'prayed theology' is a practice of growing into the likeness of God of whom, to whom and in whom one speaks.

Notes

1 Hadewijch, *Vision* Seven, in *Hadewijch: The Complete Works*, translated by Mother Columba Hart, O. S. B (New York: Paulist Press, 1980), p. 280. All English translations of Hadewijch's works are from Hart's volume. Henceforth they will be cited according to their title and page number.

2 See for example Paul Mommaers' important study, *Hadewijch: Writer, Beguine, Love Mystic* (Leuven: Peeters, 2004), ch. 6. This position is likewise held by Columba Hart in her English translation of Hadewijch's corpus, who considers these three figures to be her key sources, mentioning also Origen, Gregory the Great, and Augustine, among others. See *Hadewijch: The Complete Works*, p. 6. R. W. Southern argues that Bernard's theology and literary view shares much with Anselm's, particularly in the 'emphasis on personal experience, appeal to the individual conscience [and] delving into the roots of the inner life' (R. W. Southern, *The Making of the Middle Ages* (New Haven: Yale University Press, 1953), p. 228). Southern attributes their similarity in large part to their mutual adherence to the *Rule of Benedict*, for Anselm had little indirect and no direct influence upon the younger monk (p. 227).

3 John Arblaster and Rob Faesen, eds, *A Companion to John of Ruusbroec* (Leiden: Brill, 2014), p. 22, n. 44. See also Mary Lou Shea, *Medieval Women on Sin and Salvation: Hadewijch of Antwerp, Beatrice of Nazareth, Margaret Ebner and Julian of Norwich* (New York: Peter Lang, 2010), which examines the degree to which Anselm's soteriological position as articulated in the *Cur deus homo* was accepted by late medieval female theologians.

4 R. W. Southern, *Saint Anselm: A Portrait in a Landscape* (Cambridge: Cambridge University Press, 1990), pp. 99–112; idem, *The Making of the Middle Ages*, pp. 225–40. It is key to note that Southern is careful to say that in this 'transformation', Anselm was not inventing out of whole cloth, but giving voice to the 'spiritual currents' and 'religious impulses' of the new interests of eleventh-century piety.

5 *Cur deus homo* rejects the 'devil's rights' theory of the atonement, which holds that God tricked the devil into renouncing his justified claim on human souls by disguising himself as a human being whom the devil claimed as his own despite having not right to it, thereby losing his prerogative to all souls. Anselm argued instead that the drama was between not the devil and God but humanity and God; human beings were responsible for sin and thus were required to make restitution to God. The infinite debt was paid by a God-man, sinless yet mortal, infinite yet human, and so 'the way was now open for a fresh appreciation of the human sufferings of the Redeemer. The figure on the cross was seen with a new clarity to be that of a Man. The Devil slipped out of the drama and left God and Man face to face'. See Southern, *Making*, p. 236, on its import.

6 Cf. Augustine, *The Literal Meaning of Genesis*, Book XII, where he situates imagination below intellectual apprehension in the hierarchy of perception because of its greater corporeality (*The Literal Meaning of Genesis*, translated by John Hammond Taylor (New York: Newman Press, 1982), XII.11 p. 191).

7 Anselm, 'Meditation on Human Redemption', p. 230. English translation of *The Prayers and Meditations* and the *Proslogion*, by Benedicta Ward, OSB, *The Prayers and Meditations of Saint Anselm with the Proslogion* (London: Penguin Books, 1973). Hereafter cited as 'Ward' with page number. Critical edition by F. S. Schmitt, *S. Anselmi Cantuariensis Archiepiscopi,*

Opera Omnia, Tomus Secundus, vol. III (Stuttgart: Friedrich Frommann Verlag, 1984), p. 84. Hereafter cited as 'Schmitt', with page number.

8 Jean Leclercq, *The Love of Learning and the Desire for God*, translated by Catherine Misrahi (New York: Fordham University Press, 1961), p. 29. In monastic literature, which is, Leclercq argues, 'in large part, a literature of compunction whose aim is to possess, to increase and to communicate the desire for God', one finds God 'pressing' upon the soul (*cum-pungere*), 'piercing', or 'stinging' it in order to turn its attention to God (p. 30). On compunction in the Eastern Church, see Irénée Hausherr, *Penthos: The Doctrine of Compunction in the Christian East*, translated by Anselm Hufstader (Kalamazoo: Cistercian Publications, 1982).

9 Ward, *Prayers*, p. 101.

10 Ward, p. 184; Schmitt, II.III, p. 55.

11 Anselm, *On Truth*, ch. 13, in *Anselm of Canterbury: The Major Works*, edited by Brian Davies and G. R. Evans (Oxford: Oxford University Press, 1998), pp. 171–4; Marcia Colish, *The Mirror of Language* (New Haven: Yale University Press, 1968), p. 115.

12 Colish, *Mirror*, p. 116. See Anselm, *On Truth*, ch. 2, pp. 153–5; and Peter King, 'Anselm's Philosophy of Language', in *The Cambridge Companion to Anselm* (Cambridge: Cambridge University Press, 2004), p. 103.

13 Colish, *Mirror*, p. 115.

14 As a theologian famous for his attempts to find *a priori* proofs for the existence and nature of God, appealing to reason rather than to scripture for the authority of his arguments, Anselm has been called the 'father of scholasticism'. As the author of *The Prayers and Meditations*, Anselm has been interpreted as a mystic who seeks divine heights through the vehicle of his passions. For some, the discursive arenas in which Anselm's work takes place, one rational and systematic, the other affective and poetic, are manifestations of the two avenues available in theological investigation, paths that are mapped onto the genres that Anselm explored. For these neoscholastics, the two options are, Marcia Colish observes, 'parallel roads that never meet' (*Mirror*, pp. 86–8). For a reading of Anselm by an anti-neoscholastic author who, nevertheless, reads him as exhibiting this double nature, see Henri de Lubac's *Corpus Mysticum: The Eucharist and the Church in the Middle Ages*, translated by Gemma Simmonds, et al., edited by Laurence Paul Hemming and Susan Frank Parsons (Notre Dame: Notre Dame University Press, 2006 [1944]), p. 240.

15 For a classic treatment of Anselm that reads him non-reductively, see Leclercq, *Love of Learning*, p. 214. Leclercq argues that speculative knowledge and knowledge gained from intimate contact with God are two components of Anselm's work, sometimes articulated independently, sometimes in concert, a dynamic that makes sense for a theologian whose daily life was formed by the rhythms of Benedictine monastic life. Anselm's work thus straddles Leclercq's ideal types of scholastic and monastic theology.

16 Sweeney notes that although R. W. Southern argues that the meditation that was an essential part of Benedictine practice was a source for both private prayer and intellectual pursuits, and thus philosophical 'inquiry was scarcely distinguishable from the prayer, since the aim of both was to shake off the torpor of the mind and see things as they are in their essential being', Southern maintains that Anselm's work contains two separate trajectories, 'one descending toward the abasement of the self, the other ascending upward toward God, and they are sequential, the first, the obliteration of self-will in the prayers, which is followed by seeking knowledge of God in speculative argument'. Eileen Sweeney, *Anselm of Canterbury and the Desire for the Word* (Washington DC: Catholic University of America Press, 2012), p. 7. For Southern, see *Saint Anselm and His Biographer: A Study of Monastic Life and Thought 1059–c.1130* (Cambridge: Cambridge University Press, 1967), p. 53

17 Eileen Sweeney, *Anselm of Canterbury*, pp. 7–8.

18 Ibid., p. 36.

19 Anselm, *Proslogion*, Preface, in Ward, *The Prayers and Meditations*, p. 239.

20 See Anselm Stolz, who argues that the *Proslogion* must be read first as an address to God – an *alloquium* as it describes itself in the penultimate word of the preface. Anslem Stolz, 'Anselm's Theology in the *Proslogion*', translated by Arthur C. McGill, edited by John Hick and A. McGill, in *The Many Faced Argument* (Eugene: Wipf & Stock, 2009 [1967]), p. 200.

21 These connections seem to be why their English translator, Benedicta Ward, published them together.

22 Louis Mackey, *Peregrinations of the Word: Studies in Medieval Philosophy* (Ann Arbor: University of Michigan Press, 1997), p. 94.

23 R. A. Herrera examines the structure of the text in *Anselm's Proslogion: An Introduction* (Washington, DC: University Press of America, 1979), pp. 15–28.

24 Latin in F. S. Schmitt, O.S.B., 'Proslogion', in *S. Anselmi Cantuariensis Archiepiscopi Opera Omnia, Tomus Primus*, vol. 1 (Stuttgart: Friedrich Frommann Verlag, 1984), ch. 14, p. 111. English translation from Benedicta Ward in *The Prayers*, p. 255.

25 Colish, *Mirror*, p. 85.

26 *Proslogion*, Preface; Ward p. 238; Schmitt, I.I., p. 94.

27 Louis Mackey, *Peregrinations*, p. 81. For a helpful exposition of the difficulties of language in the *Proslogion* that includes a substantial discussion of Mackey's interpretation, see Eileen Sweeney, *Anselm*, ch. 4.

28 *Proslogion*, ch. 2; Ward, p. 244; Schmitt, I.I, p. 101.

29 To be clear, the absence of which I speak is a subjective perception, and does not refer to divine absence as an objective reality for Anselm.

30 *Proslogion*, ch. 14; Ward, p. 255; Schmitt, I.I, p. 111.

31 *Proslogion*, ch.16; Ward, pp. 257–8; Schmitt, I.I, p. 112.

32 *Proslogion*, ch.14; Ward, p. 256; Schmitt, I.I, p. 111.

33 Anselm, *On the Fall of the Devil*, in *Anselm of Canterbury: The Major Works*, ch. 14, pp. 216–17; *De Concordia*, in *Anselm of Canterbury*, ch. 3.9, pp. 464–6.

34 Anselm, *Proslogion*, ch. 17; Ward, p. 258; Schmitt, I.I, p. 113.

35 Anselm, 'Prayer to Christ', Ward, p. 94; Schmitt, II.III, p. 7.

36 Benedicta Ward, 'Preface', in *The Prayers and Meditations*, p. 17; Sweeney, *Anselm*, p. 13. The *Meditation on Human Redemption* and the treatise *Cur Deus Homo* for which it was the 'devotional counterpart' were written in 1098 (R. W. Southern, 'Foreward' in *The Prayers*, p. 14).

37 R. W. Southern, 'Foreward' in *The Prayers and Meditations*, p. 9.

38 R. W. Southern, *Saint Anselm: A Portrait*, pp. 99–112; idem, *Making*, pp. 225–40.

39 On the popularity of these works, see Thomas Bestul, *Texts of the Passion: Latin Devotional Literature and Medieval Culture* (Philadelphia: University of Pennsylvania Press, 1994), p. 36. The *Prayers and Meditations* inspired a great many imitators and Anselm's prestige as a devotional writer led to the attribution of his name to many other such works. The *Patrologia Latina* contains 75 prayers and 21 meditations under Anselm's name, a quite accurate representation of the medieval textual tradition. In the 1920s André Wilmart determined that 19 prayers and three meditations belonged to the historical Anselm. This was not, interestingly, the situation with his theological and grammatical works, which were not similarly misattributed. Bestul reconsiders the importance of such misattribution for the medieval understanding of authorship in *Texts of the Passion*, pp. 13–18.

40 Anne Clark Bartlett and Thomas H. Bestul, 'Introduction', in *Cultures of Piety: Medieval English Devotional Literature in Translation* (Ithaca: Cornell University Press, 1999), p. 2; T. Bestul, *Texts of the Passion*, p. 35; Jean Leclercq, 'Sur la devotion à l'humanité du Christ', *Revue Benedictine* 63 (1953), pp. 128–30; R. W. Southern, *Making*, pp. 232–40. Southern argues that with Fransciscan popularization, the Anselmian transformation entered the marketplace, becoming the 'common property of the lay and clerical world alike' (Southern, *Making*, p. 240). Later scholars have questioned the timeline of the Southern thesis, arguing that intense affective piety is apparent in ninth-century

Anglo Saxon literature. For example, Allen Frantzen, 'Spirituality and Devotion in the Anglo-Saxon Penitentials', *Essays in Medieval Studies* 22 (2005), pp. 117–28. Michael Sargent notes that affective devotional practices were part of *lectio divina* of late antiquity ('Introduction' to *Nicholas Love: The Mirror of the Blessed Life of Jesus Christ: A Reading Text* (Exeter: Exeter University Press, 2005), p. x). We will see that the tradition of *lectio divina* is indeed crucial for Anselm's *The Prayers and Meditations*. The claim that there are historical precedents for works like Anselm's prayers or affective piety more broadly does not, however, discount the argument that there was a shift in emphasis and intensity in the eleventh century.

41   Ward, p. 107; Schmidt, II.III, p. 13.
42   *Proslogion*, ch. 16; Ward, p. 258; Schmitt, I.I, p. 113.
43   Ward, p. 108; Schmitt, II.III, p. 13.
44   English translation here by R. W. Southern in *Saint Anselm*, p. 100; Schmitt, II.III, p. 30.
45   Ward, p. 188; Schmitt, II.III, p. 57–8.
46   The connections with Book VII of *Confessions*, in which Augustine struggles to undergo a conversion of the will that is congruent with his conversion to the 'certainty' of the content of faith is clear. Anselm argued that the will had two different dispositions or orientations that are irreducible. One is a desire for happiness and the other for rectitude. In the prelapsarian context, the former submitted to the latter. After the fall, the two were no longer aligned. This disjunction created a disturbance in the will that is painful. See Robert Pouchet, *La Rectitudo chez Saint Anselme: Un Itinéraire Augustinien de L'Âme a Dieu* (Paris: Études Augustiniennes, 1964), pp. 193–4; *De Concordia* in *Anselm of Canterbury: The Major Works*, 3.11, pp. 467–70; 3.13, p. 471.
47   Ward, p. 188; Schmitt, II.III, p. 57.
48   Anselm, *Why God Became Man*, in *Anselm of Canterbury*, 1.19–20, pp. 300–305; Schmitt I.II, pp. 84–8.
49   Anselm, *Why God Became Man*, 2.18–19, pp. 348–54; Schmitt I.II, pp. 126–31.
50   Such scripts and the work required to appropriate doctrine and reorient the will are required after baptism, for even though baptism removes injustice from the soul, pain remains, Anselm notes, so that a person might create the merit that leads to a state of beatitude that arrives after death. The work of spiritual discipline is one of 'submit[ting] to the ordeal of our liberty'. Beatitude is the 'reward of our voluntary effort in cooperation with divine grace (Pouchet, *La Rectitudo*, p. 191. Cf. *De Concordia*, 3.9, pp. 464–6; and 3.12, pp. 470–71).
51   For a consideration of the import of their formal aspect, see Southern, 'Foreword' in *The Prayers*, pp. 9–15.
52   'Prayer to St John the Baptist', Ward, p. 130; Schmitt, II.III, p. 27.
53   Ward, p. 95; Schmitt, II.III, p. 7.
54   'Prayer to Christ', Ward, p. 94; Schmitt, II.III, p. 7.
55   Ward, p. 230; Schmitt, II.III, p. 84.
56   Ward, p. 230; Schmitt, II.III, p. 84.
57   Cassian, *Conferences*, translated by Boniface Ramsey, O.P. (New York: Newman Press, 1997), X.11, p. 384. The source of late ancient theology was this prayerful, meditative reading, and between theology and prayer there was no distinction (Benedicta Ward, 'Introduction', to *The Prayers and Meditations*, p. 44). Anselm received this tradition of prayed theology through *The Rule of Benedict*. Benedict not only conveyed the teaching of John Cassian (ca. 360–435) on prayer, but prescribed his works in chapters 42.3; 42.5 and 73.5. See Benedict of Nursia, *The Rule of St. Benedict 1980*, edited by Timothy Frye, O.S.B. (Collegeville, MN: The Liturgical Press 1981).
58   See for example, Augustine, *De civitate Dei* 20.10; *De Trinitate* 5.2.3; *Confessions* 6.1, 10.40.65, 11.11.13. Bernard of Clairvaux, for whom Ps. 33:9 is a favourite verse, considers the sensory contact with the divine described by the Psalmist as indicating the intimate, affective contact with God experienced in contemplation. This 'tasting' of divinity

fills the soul with wisdom, and Bernard frequently employs the wordplay of *sapere/ sapientia* to speak of the wisdom that comes from *unitas spiritus*, the knowledge of God that is found in 'the wine of contemplation'. See Gordon Rudy, *The Mystical Language of Sensation in the Later Middle Ages* (New York: Routledge, 2002), p. 62. Rudy's study also examines the language of sensation in Hadewijch, for whom he argues the language of tasting and touching indicates 'immediate' and 'reciprocal' contact with other bodies (p. 67).

59 The terms appear together in the *Monologion*, ch. 44 when Anselm argues that it is not contradictory to maintain that the Son exists both through his own essence and is begotten of the Father's essence. They also appear in the 'Letter on the Sacrifice of the Leavened and Unleavened bread', used not to indicate the nature of the encounter with God, but as a polemical invocation of Romans 12:3 regarding the interpretation and enactment of Christ's words. See 'Epistola de sacrificio azimi et fermentati', in Schmitt, *Opera Omnia*, II, p. 226. Anselm quotes Psalm 33:9 in his letter to Haimonem and Rainaldum, a letter whose language and tone is profoundly reminiscent of *The Prayers and Meditations*. See Schmitt, *Opera Omnia*, Vol. III, p. 120.

60 For example, in the 'Prayer to Paul', Paul is called *dulcis nutrix* and *dulcis mater* (Schmitt, *Opera Omnia* III, p. 39). In the 'Prayer to Mary', Mary is *dulcis*, a sweet force that can 'liquefy' the soul and make the spirit sweet (*dulcedine*). Ibid, p. 24. Benedict, a *suavis magister* and *dulcis pater*, teaches *suavis doctrina* and *dulcis admonitio*. Ibid., p. 62.

61 The language of sweetness is common, for example, in Augustine, for whom it often has Christological connotations. Through Christ the bitter nature (*amarus*) of human life in its alienation from God is made 'sweet' (*suavis*). *Sermones de Scripturis*, sermon 145.5, *Patrologia Latina* 38.794; *Ennarrationes in Psalmos*, 'In psalmum CXXXIV', par. 5, *Patrologia Latina* 37.1741–1742. See Ella Johnson, 'To Taste (*sapere*) Wisdom (*sapientia*): Eucharistic Devotion in the Writings of Gertrude of Helfta', *Viator* 44, no. 2 (2013), p. 179; Rachel Fulton, 'Taste and See that the Lord is Sweet' (Ps. 33:9): the Flavor of God in the Monastic West', *Journal of Religion* 86 (2006), pp. 169–204 (p. 177, p. 182).

62 Ella Johnson, 'To Taste (*sapere*) Wisdom (*sapientia*)', p. 175. For recent studies of the tradition of the spiritual senses, see Paul L. Gavrilyuk and Sarah Coakley, eds, *The Spiritual Senses: Perceiving God in Western Christianity* (Cambridge: Cambridge University Press, 2012); Rachel Fulton, 'Taste and See'; Rosemary Drage Hale, '"Taste and See, for God is Sweet": Sensory Perception and Memory in Medieval Christian Mystical Experience', in *Vox Mystica: Essays on Medieval Mysticism in Honor of Professor Valerie M. Lagorio*, ed. Anne Clark Bartlett et al. (Cambridge: D. S. Brewer, 1995), pp. 3–14; Gordon Rudy, *The Mystical Language of Sensation in the Later Middle Ages* (New York: Routledge, 2002); John C. Cavadini, 'The Sweetness of the Word: Salvation and Rhetoric in Augustine's *De doctrina christiana*', in *De doctrina christiana: a Classic of Western Culture*, ed. Duane W. H. Arnold and Pamela Bright (South Bend: University of Notre Dame Press, 1995), pp. 164–81.

63 Ward, p. 101; Schmitt, II.III, p. 10.

64 On identifying Hadewijch see Rob Faesen, 'Was Hadewijch a Beguine or a Cistercian?', *Cîteaux: Revue d'Histoire Cistercienne* 55 (2004), pp. 47–63.

65 For a discussion of models from troubadour songs and hymns for five of the *Poems in Stanzas*, see Louis P. Grijp, 'De zingende Hadewijch', in Frank Willaert, ed., *Een zoet akkoord. Middeleeuwse lyriek in de Lage Landen* (Amsterdam: Prometheus, 1992), pp. 72–93. See also Anikó Daróczi, *Hadewijch. Ende hieromme swighic sachte* (Amsterdam-Antwerp: Atlas, 2002), who argues the *Letters* were used in ritual settings in which oration was interspersed with song. Cited by Veerle Fraeters, 'Foreword', in Paul Mommaers with Elizabeth Dutton, *Hadewijch: Writer-Beguine-Love Mystic* (Leuven: Peeters, 2004), p. x.

66 On the education of women in the Low Countries in the high Middle Ages, see Walter Simons, *Cities of Ladies: Beguine Communities in the Low Countries, 1200–1565* (Philadelphia: University of Pennsylvania Press, 2001).

67 Mommaers with Elzabeth Dutton, *Hadewijch: Writer-Beguine-Love Mystic*, p. 4. On Hadewijch's adaptation of both troubadour and biblical traditions, see Barbara Newman, 'Thirteenth-Century Beguines and the Art of Love', in Newman, *From Virile Women to Woman-Christ: Studies in Medieval Religion and Literature* (Philadelphia: University of Pennsylvania Press, 1995), pp. 137–67.

68 Hadewijch, *Brieven*, edited by J. Van Mierlo (Antwerp: Standaard-Boekhandel, 1947), vol. 1, p. 51.

69 Hadewijch, *Letter Six*, p. 63. Love (*minne*) is 'everything' for Hadewijch and thus can be a remarkably flexible word, an ambiguity she exploits. Following 1 John 4:16, *minne* is God, either in a general sense or identified with the Son or Holy Spirit, and as such is used as a proper noun. *Minne* is also a divine power suffusing the created universe, and thus speaks of the force of the madness (*orwoet*) of love. As Bernard McGinn notes, for human beings, 'love is both the experience of being subjected to this overpowering force and our response to it, the power of our own activity of loving that brings us to God.' (*The Flowering of Mysticism: Men and Women in the New Mysticism, 1200–1350* (New York: Crossroad, 1998), p. 202). It may refer, then, to God's love for human beings or the soul's response to God, itself rooted in the original divine love such that the love with which the soul loves God is God's love and that love is God. The *Poem in Couplets* 15 uses this lability to create a dizzying referential map, defeating distinctions between object, subject, the same and the other:

> 'O love, were I love And with love to love you, love O love, for love grant that love May know love wholly as love' (p. 352, l. 49–52).

70 Hadewijch, *Letter Six*, pp. 62–3.324. This reference was first noted by John Arblaster and Rob Faesen in *A Companion to John of Ruusbroec*, p. 22, n. 44.

71 *Letter Six*, p. 58.86.

72 *Letter Six*, p. 58.102. cf. *Why God Became Man*, 1.12, p. 284–5; 2.20, p. 354.

73 *Vision One*, p. 268–9.

74 *Vision One*, p. 269–70.

75 Hart, 'Introduction', in *Hadewijch: The Complete Works*, p. 4.

76 In this focus on the whole of Christ's life, Hadewijch, too, is being Anselmian. It has been a common critique of the *CDH*, inspired by Gustav Aulén's influential work, *Christus Victor*, that Anselm focuses on Christ's death to the detriment of his entire incarnate existence. Anselm's stated purpose in writing the *CDH*, however, is to provide necessary reasons for the incarnation. He thus claims that there are many reasons in addition to his death 'why it will be extremely appropriate for him to bear a resemblance to [human beings] and to have the behaviour belonging to [humankind] – while being without sin' (2.11, p. 331). The treatise, moreover, contains a chapter that considers 'how by Christ's life restitution is made to God for human sins' (2.18, p. 348). See Gavin Ortlund, 'On the Throwing of Rocks: An Objection to Hasty and Un-Careful Criticisms of Anselm's Doctrine of the Atonement', *The Saint Anselm Journal* 8.2 (Spring 2013), pp. 4–8, for an elaborate articulation of this position.

77 *Letter* Six, p. 61.249.

78 Ibid., p. 62.274.

79 Ibid., p. 57.19.

80 '*deen vor dander.*' *Letter One*, p. 47; see Rob Faesen, 'Hadewijch's Eucharistic *Vision 7–8* Reconsidered', in *The Materiality of Devotion in Late Medieval Northern Europe: Images, Objects, Practices*, ed. Hening Laugerud, et al. (Dublin: Four Courts Press, 2016), p. 37.

81 *Letter* Ten, p. 68.51.

82 Ibid., p. 67.26.

83 *Letter Six*, p. 61.227.

84 Ibid., p. 59.117–28.

85 Arblaster and Faesen, eds., *A Companion to John of Ruusbroec*, p. 23.

86 *Letter* Six, p. 57.19.

87 *Vision* One, pp. 270–71.

88 *Letter* Seventeen, p. 84.101.

89 Paul Mommaers, S.J., *The Riddle of Christian Mystical Experience: The Role of the Humanity of Jesus* (Leuven: Peeters, 2002), p. 180.

90 Rob Faesen thus calls it a feast of deification. See 'Hadewijch's Eucharistic *Vision 7–8*', p. 37.

91 *Vision* Seven, p. 280.

92 *Vision* Seven, pp. 281–2.

93 Bernard McGinn argues that in Hadewijch one finds one of the first examples of the notion of union without distinction, later given explicit articulation by Meister Eckhart and others. This understanding of union goes beyond earlier understandings of *unitas spiritus*, in which union is conceived of as a joining, through love, of an infinite with a finite Spirit. In Hadewijch one finds such descriptions alongside a conception of the eternal, exemplary soul present in the abyss of the Trinity before the existence of a 'created nature', in which the soul is permanently grounded and by virtue of which it enjoys a union without distinction (see *Visions* Eleven and Twelve). Thus in *Letter* Eighteen Hadewijch writes of God and the soul as 'mutual abysses, equally bottomless in the power of *Minne*'. These two infinite abysses are, in fact one, sharing a kiss 'with one single mouth' (*Poems in Couplets* 12). Bernard McGinn, *Flowering*, pp. 214–17.

94 Faesen, 'Hadewijch's Eucharistic *Vision 7–8*', p. 42. Faesen likens it to the stigmata of Francis, Elizabeth of Spalbeek, and Ida of Leuven.

95 Ibid., p. 42.

96 Anselm, *Why God Became Man*, 1.20, pp. 303–5.

97 Mommaers, 'Preface', in Hart, p. xxii.

98 *Poems in Couplets* 16, 149–62, p. 356.

99 *Letter* Twelve, pp. 70.40.

100 *Letter* Eight, p. 65.27.

101 Ibid.

102 Mommaers, *Riddle*, p. 180. Mommaers argues that one may trace the transformation of *ghebreken* into *gheliken*, from lack and failure to a 'being like' Christ, from *Vision* One to *Vision* Seven. See also *Letter* Thirteen: 'What satisfies Love best of all is that we be wholly destitute of all repose, whether in aliens, or in friends, or even in Love herself. And this is a frightening life Love wants, that we must do without the satisfaction of Love in order to satisfy Love…' (p. 75.34).

103 Mommaers, *Riddle*, p. 180.

104 McGinn, *Flowering*, pp. 214–17.

105 Columba Hart notes the consonance of Hadewijch's theology of eternal progress with Gregory of Nyssa's ('Introduction', in *Hadewijch: The Complete Works*, p. 7). Likewise, Bernard McGinn argues that with Hadewijch and other representative of the 'new mysticism' of the thirteenth century, one finds a notion of *epektasis* (*Flowering*, p. 220).

106 *Letter* Eight, p. 65.27.

107 The question of whether or not Hadewijch read the *Proslogion* is the subject of another investigation that I shall not pursue here.

108 *Vision* Fourteen, p. 305.

8 Etching the ineffable in words

The return of contemplation to theology

Martin Laird, O.S.A.

Introduction

Some years ago I was speaking with a friend who is a rising star in her field of theology. I knew that she was coming up for tenure and a promotion in rank at her university. Yet, somehow, everything about her demeanour, affect, her pallid complexion, suggested the sinister rattle of depression/anxiety. I asked, 'So, how's life?' She sat down and began to sob.

The stakes are high in most American universities. Application for tenure and rank are conjoined. If one's application for tenure and promotion from the lower rank of assistant professor to the higher rank of associate professor does not go through, one is sacked (not on the spot; one has a year of teaching, with benefits, as well as time to look for another job, sulk or sue). To make matters worse, the lead-up to finding out if one has both received tenure and merited promotion in rank is carried out in complete secrecy at every level. One is allowed to know neither who referees one's dossier nor what is said about the dossier. These things one will never find out. What 'Rank and Tenure' committees at various levels of university administration are saying about one, is by way of academic policy, kept completely secret. My friend was in a state of limbo. Pope Benedict XVI may have deleted limbo from Roman Catholic teaching on the afterlife, but limbo is alive and well in American academia.

She finally began to speak about what had initially drawn her to pursue doctoral studies in theology: 'I did it because I thought God was calling me to a life of scholarship and prayer, and that teaching at the university level was a way of responding to a vocation. But now this vocation is being bureaucratized out of me'. Does academia allow for theology as a vocation or must such a vocation be thrown to the colosseum amidst the spectacle of backbiting, gossip, and careerism?

It was obvious to me that she had not lost her vocation, but was suffering from the deracinating manoeuvres that dominate the academy. This deafens the ear of the deep listening required to perceive the vocation to theology as a way of living life in God and of living out that life in service of the deeply humane desire to know. As Aristotle expressed it so long ago: 'Every person by nature desires to know.'[1] Theology as a vocation (and not merely one's job) risks desiccation to the point that we do not so much live as choke on the dust of careerism. Careerism deveins vocation. Surely, this is something of what R. S. Thomas was getting at in his poem, 'Of Theologians':

> The word as an idea,
> Crumbled by their dry minds in long sentences
> Of their chapters, gathering dust
> In their libraries; a sacrament that,
> If not soon swallowed, sticks in the throat.[2]

In his poem 'I Apologize', Czeslaw Milosz speaks with thinly veiled cynicism of his own inability to take seriously theology's verbose din:

> I apologize, most reverend theologians, for a tone not befitting the purple of your robes.
> ...
> If even gray-haired theologians concede that it is too much for them, close the book, and invoke the inadequacy of the human tongue.[3]

The purpose of this essay is to explore how representative, authoritative theologians (saints and doctors of the church in the Roman Catholic tradition) presume that the life of inner stillness, leading to contemplation, is an essential, normative component of the practice of theology, if not the very ground of its seeking, which together form a theological life. What does this essay mean by 'a theological life'? In this context, it means a way of life so grounded in inner stillness that this life becomes a servant of the Word and, hence, is forever attempting to etch the ineffable in vowels and virtues for the well-being of others. Moreover, how does contemplation, both deep and deeply integrating, change the way life looks to the contemplative? Because this approach, bearing as it does on certain key concerns of theology, might sound rather shocking to some theologians whose dusty sentences 'get stuck in the throat', I shall base my argument on those theologians in the Christian tradition whose authority has been well established.

St. Gregory the Theologian and the ocean's calm

The fourth-century St. Gregory the Theologian, also called St. Gregory Nazianzen,[4] has, like my theologian friend, similar problems with the way the theological life is (not) lived and practised, especially by a group of theologians called the Eunomians, named so after their leader, Eunomius.[5] In one of Gregory's best-known orations, *Oration* 27, he takes issue with the Eunomians on this very point. In the process of challenging their lop-sided Trinitarian theology, he says what he thinks is wrong with their way of going about theology beginning with their methodology, and in the process Gregory enunciates a sort of plan of formation for training one who truly wants to take up theology in such a way that it becomes a way of life.

The audience of this *Oration* is a group of Arian hangers-on, who basically hold that the Word, the second Person of the Trinity, incarnate in Jesus, is not God in the same way that the Father is God or the Holy Spirit is God. They were what are called subordinationists.[6] But, for our purposes, what is fascinating is that Gregory sees that the roots of their problems are their lack of proper theological formation. What are their problems and what is the required theological formation enunciated by Gregory Nazianzen? The problem with the Eunomians, which doubtless undergirds their heterodox views on God, is their 'itching ears' (1 Tim 4:3).[7] Both their tongues and their hands also itch and are ready to go on the attack, in this case against Gregory himself.[8] They also suffer from their 'delight in profane and vain babblings and contradictions ...'.[9] Gregory calls this contradictory babbling, 'elaborate verbiage'.[10] Disordered desire and empty babbling are going to skew from the outset, in Gregory's view, their approach to the very possibility of encountering God and, therefore, their practice of theology. As a result of their empty, obsessive chatter, he claims 'they have undermined every approach to true religion by their complete obsession with solving conundrums. They are like promoters of wrestling bouts in the theatres.'[11] It is sheer spectacle that does not even follow the rules. Moreover, he says, they are not content until 'every square in the city buzzes with their arguments, every party must be made tedious by their boring nonsense'.[12] Gregory has identified their problem; they talk too much. They delight in idle babbling and elaborate verbiage. This undermines the proper formation of theology and reduces theology to idle chatter, violence and competition as a way of life. Gregory now lets up on his critique and proceeds (1) to make some observations about the practice of theology, and (2) to delineate a simple programme of theological formation.

First, he declares that the 'discussion of theology is not for everyone. I tell you, not for everyone—it is no such inexpensive or effortless pursuit. Nor ... is it for every occasion, and certain limits must be observed.'[13] Who, then, is the right person? When is the appropriate occasion? Who is the suitable audience? The right person is someone who has not simply a sound footing in study, but more importantly, he says, they 'have undergone, or at the very least are undergoing, purification of body and soul'.[14] The appropriate time is whenever the commanding faculty of the mind, the *hegemónikon*, is decluttered of 'confusing, illusory, wandering images' .... And, finally, Gregory comes out with it: 'We actually need to be still in order to know God.'[15] He finds the exegetical grounding for the possibility of theology as spiritual practice in Ps 46:10: 'Be still and know that I am God.'

Who is the proper audience to listen to discussions of theology? Gregory suggests that it is those who have undergone a similar inner purification and consider theology not just one more topic to talk about, 'like', he claims, 'any other entertaining small talk after the races, the theatre, ... for there are people who count chatter about theology and clever deployment of arguments as one of their amusements'.[16] Note that for Gregory the Theologian, both the person who *speaks* on theological topics and the person who *listens* to them, must already be living a life that involves the purification/simplification of both body and mind. Hence, there is a certain way of life involved in the practice of theology, from either direction. What does he mean by purification of the body? – 'Showing hospitality; admiring brotherly love; spousal affection; virginity; feeding the poor; singing psalms; fasting.'[17] You will also have noted that these practices draw us deeper into the life of a praying, socially engaged community. The inner purification focuses on drawing into stillness the obsessive preoccupation with inner chatter that deafens us to everything but the inner chatter. This inner chatter is responsible for two perils for the theologian-in-formation. It sets loose the wagging tongue and leads to competition in theological matters. Only after this radical uncluttering of the mind are we able to look at ourselves. Taking obvious inspiration from one of the greatest of spiritual masters, Plotinus, Gregory tells us to 'look at ourselves and to smooth the theologian in us, like a statue, into beauty'.[18]

After these bodily and spiritual practices, which help form the character of the theologian, Gregory asks in *Oration* 28: What is the right occasion to practise theology? 'The right occasion', he says, 'is when we possess a vast, inner stillness'.[19] It is worth noting the Greek word Gregory uses here for stillness: *galēnos*. The term suggests the still calm of the ocean as well as essential nuances of depth and vastness.

For Gregory the Theologian, then, the training of a theologian requires the following: the purification (or simplification) of the body in such a way that we are more deeply drawn into Christian community, as well as a mind decluttered of inner noise. Moreover, this programme of theological formation implies what we might call the practice of contemplation, which, if practised to full-flowering, facilitates the bathing in light of the human structures of knowing in which the illusion of separation between God and the human is seen through. While Gregory does not expand on this in the two *Orations* we have considered, it is the *primary* concern of the contemplative training we find in Gregory's friend, Evagrius Ponticus. Evagrius gives us a close look at what is at issue in the purification of the mind.

'Let stillness be the criterion for testing the value of everything'

The fourth-century monk of the Egyptian desert, Evagrius Ponticus, provides a good opportunity to consider these things in closer detail.[20] Not simply because Evagrius and Gregory Nazianzen come from the same Roman Province of Cappadocia, where the two were old acquaintances, nor because Evagrius proved a talented administrative assistant of sorts when Gregory spent a brief period as Patriarch of Constantinople. It is, rather, on his keen psychological and spiritual insight that we will be focusing here.

Evagrius was the first great desert psychologist and, in a manner typical of fourth-century contemplative psychology, often expresses his penetrating insight in the language of the demons. In a work written for early training in the contemplative life, *The Praktikos*, Evagrius sets out in greater detail than Gregory the simplifying dynamics of still prayer. The focus is primarily on the ordeal with afflictive thoughts (*logismoi)* and their way of targeting what Evagrius termed *pathos* (I shall leave the word untranslated and focus instead on how *pathos* seems to work). To describe *pathos* in contemporary language, we could say that it involves deeply ingrained mental habits of obsession. The more indulged it is the greater its momentum and resulting cluttering of aware-ness. But, there needs to be something to set *pathos* off. This is the role of the afflictive thought (*logismos*). There seems to be something especially grasping about the character of *pathos*. You might say that *pathos* is something like the hook-side of a Velcro strip. It is always ready to grasp onto something. The graspable side of the strip consists of certain afflictive thoughts, which Evagrius famously groups into eight types.[21] The demon's role is to introduce to the obsessive hooks of the *pathos* various afflictive thoughts (*logismoi*). These afflic-tive thoughts, working either alone or teaming up together (there are various strategies deployed) in such a way as to get *pathos* worked up into a frenzied state of obsessive grasping. The result of this is the lightening-quick production of an inner video of sorts, to which our attention is completely riveted. They may be pleasant, silly or painful. It does not matter what sort of inner video is produced. The demon's desire is that our attention be completely stolen by them and, as Evagrius says, 'we run to see them'.[22] The key dynamic is this: the chattering noise in the mind is produced when the *pathos* latches on to the afflictive thought. And as long as the contemplative's attention is riveted to this inner world of incessant, scheming, confusing chatter, the demon's job is done; for the contemplative's attention is blinded to his or her innermost depths, where our life is hidden with Christ in God (Col 3:3). Instead of an inner sense of Gregory's ocean stillness, there is a backed-up sink of gunge, with the result that we remain essentially ignorant of ourselves and likewise of God. Without this cultivated, inner vigilance this incessant inner chatter can last for a short while or it can last for decades on end, enough time for an entirely closeted identity, lifestyle, or career to be constructed out of what is essentially noise-driven ambition and inner confusion. We, moreover, are left with the convinc-ing illusion that we are separate from God who needs to be sought after like some object we desire but lack.

What is Evagrius's antidote? His aim is to encourage the opening up from within successive levels of stillness to allow *pathos* to loosen its grip; to get *pathos* out from behind the wheel of the car; to quieten the yapping inner chatter of frenzied chaos that we live out of a good deal of the time. Inner stillness is revealed to be something that has always been present by means of two funda-mental dynamics: awareness and release.

In Chapters 43 and 50 of *The Praktikos*, Evagrius presents a concise and concentrated programme of cultivating awareness. He writes, 'If there are any among you who wish … to gain experience in this contemplative craft, keep careful watch over your thoughts.'[23] Evagrius wants us to have enough awareness so as to observe everything about these afflictive thoughts. He continues with this language of awareness: 'observe their intensity, their periods of decline and follow them as they rise and fall …'. 'The demons', he says, 'become infuriated with those who practise [awareness] in a manner that is increasingly contemplative'.[24] The demons become infuriated because the contemplative is becoming free 'like a sparrow from the snare of the fowler (Ps 91:3)'. Why is this so? What is the cultivation of awareness doing? It gets us out of the inner noise and cluttered narrative going on in our heads. The inner narrative does not begin until *pathos* has latched onto the afflictive thought. This happens with lightning-fast speed. Take anger, for example. Normally we are not aware of simple anger at all. Instead we are aware of the story, the *inner commentary* on what or whom we are angry at. Evagrius is suggesting that we meet the thought with stillness (a stillness deeper than our running commentaries), before *pathos* has a chance to get its hooks into it and immediately whisk up a story *about* the anger, the pride or the vainglory. You see the thought as just a thought. The inner video is a step removed. *Pathos* is the film producer here and *logismos* provides the script. It requires deep inner awareness or silence (two sides of a coin really) to excavate enough inner spaciousness to see and identify the thought before the story *about* the thought is whisked up, and we begin to suffer as a result. Enough practice softens over time the hooks of *pathos* so that instead of grasping it receives without the frantic, anxious frenzy. The gradual loosening of these grasping tentacles gives birth to what Evagrius calls *apátheia*, a deep calm that results from the harmonious integration of the emotions and gives birth to love.[25] Among Evagrius's most evocative descriptions of his, decidedly non-stoic, understanding of *apátheia* is found in *Praktikos* Chapter 64: 'The proof of *apátheia* is had when the spirit begins to see its own light … and when it maintains its calm even as it beholds all the affairs of life.'[26]

Another essential component of this contemplative training is something that Evagrius must have known about: the use of the quiet repetition of a prayer word or phrase. As we read in the Prologue to another training manual of his called *Talking Back* (*Antirrhetikos*), it seems that the desert monastic observed how Jesus dealt with evil thoughts during his temptation in the desert.[27] Instead of getting caught up in conversation with Satan, Jesus in fact interrupts this inner conversation by quoting Scripture (see Mt 4:1–10). Evagrius has endless suggestions of Scriptural phrases to repeat for any type of thought imaginable,[28] but the early contemplative tradition soon took up some form of the Jesus Prayer.[29] St. John Klimakos says: 'Let the name of Jesus cling to your every breath, and you will know the meaning of stillness.'[30] The quiet repetition of the name of Jesus as the heart of the practice of contemplation, unites us with the divinizing humanity of Jesus and ushers us into the life of the Trinity.

Through the contemplative softening of *pathos*'s grip, which otherwise dominates how life is going to look to us, Evagrius provides us with a more detailed look at what Gregory the Theologian might well mean by the purification of the theologian. The education of *pathos* leads us to Evagrius's simple description of imageless prayer, what we might call contemplative prayer.[31]

In his treatise, *Chapters on Prayer*, Evagrius describes prayer as 'the communion of the spirit (*nous*) with God'.[32] Chapter 70 also offers a definition of contemplative prayer that should be read in tandem with Chapter 3: 'Prayer is the letting go of thoughts.'[33] What is at issue here is some technical epistemological terminology; in other words, different ways of knowing. The one involves the grasp of conceptual knowing (*dianoia*), the other, the ungrasping, concept-free, open palms of unknowing (*nous*). In Chapter 70, Evagrius is referring to concepts, images and the results of all of discursive thinking. These could all fit under the umbrella of the Greek work *dianoia*. When Evagrius describes prayer as the communion of the spirit (*nous*) with God, the translator is using the word *nous* or one of its synonyms. *Nous* betokens a different cognitive state from dianoia. *Nous* has no need of concepts, but is characterized by an intuitive encounter with God not mediated by concepts, images or thoughts. In this cognitive state the awareness of a knowing subject versus a known object disappears, as Kallistos Ware has put it.[34]

We need a cognitive faculty that operates irrespective of objects because God is not an object. It is precisely this human cognitive faculty, *nous*, which is cultivated and graciously opens up from within and flowers as imageless contemplation. Sometimes the imageless contemplation of *nous* (spirit) falls like dew on the conceptual faculties, because the human cognitive faculties work in harmony, bedewing them with theological insight or a sense of interior spaciousness. Evagrius says, when we are 'filled with reverence and joy at the same time, then you can be sure that you are drawing near that open countryside whose name is prayer'.[35] This fullness of mind (*nous*) leads Evagrius to claim that imageless prayer 'is the highest act of the mind'.[36] The transfigured mind of the contemplative constitutes the unity of prayer and theology; hence, Evagrius famously says, 'If you are a theologian you truly pray. If you truly pray you are a theologian.'[37] And so we return to Gregory the Theologian.

Theology is not for everyone. With the help of Evagrius we see that it involves a graced transfiguration of the mind. Thus, for the contemplative-become-theologian, *life looks different*. When that fullness of mind, having let go of all concepts, transcends subject/object dualism, life in God offers a different perspective. Utterances of what life in God is like can sound rather shocking to the ears of the one clinging to the wedge between knower and known; one is not, to use Gregory's words, ready for theology. By contrast, one who sees with the 'eye of the heart', as Augustine puts it, perceives life differently. In this final section, then, let us look briefly at some statements by other saints and doctors of the church.

The eye of the heart

In Book 7 of *Confessions*, St. Augustine speaks movingly of his own awakening in God with the result that he saw things anew: 'unknown to me you caressed my head, and when you closed my eyes ... I began for a little while to forget myself, and my madness was lulled to sleep. When I awoke in you, I saw you differently, infinite in every sense. But what I saw was not with the eye of the body.'[38] The eye of the body would naturally be concerned with an object perceived by a knowing subject. Augustine, as others before and after him, intends a different cognitive faculty, the 'eye of the heart'. St. Augustine says that the 'entire purpose of the Christian life is to awaken the eye of the heart whereby God may be seen'.[39] What Augustine is calling the 'eye of the heart' (in fact Augustine has a host of terms for this) is a seeing, if you will, that transcends any sort of subject–object dualism. This faculty of knowing (or unknowing) has been called many things throughout history. *The Chaldaean Oracles* calls it the 'fire of the mind'. For Plotinus, it is 'the crest of the wave of *nous*'. For St. Gregory of Nyssa, in certain contexts, this unitive faculty was simply faith (*pistis*). For St. Thomas Aquinas '*ratio superior*', for others the *scintilla animae* or *apex mentis*. Though the terminology may change down through the centuries, the point is: theologians understand that there is a faculty of the mind that has a name and a function: union with God beyond all concept and image, but which union bathes the thinking mind with the light of Wisdom. Owing to this state of transfigured human awareness, where the human leaves off is simply not so obvious to the person and the divine takes up (while for subsequent, discursive theological reflection, it may be pellucid). Where precisely does the Thames cease to be the Thames and become entirely the North Sea? Where precisely does the North Sea's reach into the Thames cease to be North Sea no more?

Any number of saints, many of them Doctors of the Church, speak out of this epistemological transformation in ways that can sound a bit startling to those who only know discursive awareness, those who, according to Gregory the Theologian, are not yet ready for theology (even if they are ready for promotion in rank and tenure).

St. Catherine of Genoa (1447–1510) is well known for her startling realization of her identity. Not simply the knowledge of herself as a Genoese woman; a woman born into the noble Fieschi family; a woman caught in a bad marriage to a man who was constantly verbally abusive; a woman dedicated to care of the sick, especially to victims of the plague that ravaged the city (1497–1501). She knew her burning zeal for God. This discursive, conceptual knowledge she had in abundance. But, when she attempts to express in discursive language what is glimpsed in the unitive awareness of the 'eye of the heart', listen to what she must do with language in order to bring it as close as possible to what is beyond all words and concepts even while all words and concepts are supersaturated with Presence. She writes, 'In my soul I see nothing but God'. She is well aware that if she goes around speaking like this people won't understand the truth-claim she is making. Or she might just be burned at the stake. Yet if she is going to say things the way she perceives them in Light of the unitive awareness of the eye of the heart, then she feels she must put it this way: 'Inwardly I say: my "me" is God; nor do I know any other "me" but my God.'[40] Interestingly she does not use the word 'self' as English translations do; she uses the first person pronoun in an oblique case. She is at pains to etch the ineffable in vowels. This is what the depths of identity would call its *patria*, our native homeland. Lest the theological thought-police start applying for a warrant for the arrest of a collapsed creation theology, may I suggest that this is a statement proclaiming a full and fulfilling realization of our created identity in God.

Etching the ineffable in vowels: the problem is attempting to shoehorn into the discursive subtleties of language that which blossoms from the non-discursive flowering of human knowing, the unitive awareness of the eye of the heart. It overflows into words that leak meaning and find it difficult to contain all that is given, and so her language is going to sound catechetically untidy. This has to do with epistemological transfiguration, not collapsed theological anthropology. The non-discursive human faculty for encountering what is beyond the grasp of concepts, images and speech has been awakened, and something is always lost in the translation from the non-discursive to the discursive. Waves of ocean wash onto the shores of perception and language, but not all the ocean washes onto these shores.

It is impossible to pin words onto unitive awareness, but let us look at two Doctors of the Church, from among very many possibilities, who are well positioned to help us see this by virtue of their own realization of their lives 'hidden with Christ in God' (Col 3:3); that is, their own readiness for theology as Gregory the Theologian would have it: St. Teresa of Avila and St. John of the Cross.

St. Teresa's *Interior Castle* helps us understand how the unitive awareness of a maturing contemplative presents itself to the discursive faculties of perception, that is, when the illusion of separation has dropped. In the Seventh Dwelling, which is mostly concerned with service to one's neighbour, she says:

> In total union no separation is possible. The [person] remains perpetually in that centre ... [It] is like rain falling from the sky into a river or pool. There is nothing but water. It is impossible to divide the sky-water from the land water. When a little stream enters the sea, who could separate its waters back out again? Think of a bright light pouring into a room from two large windows: it enters from different places but becomes one light.[41]

Long before her, St. Augustine insists that 'This light itself is one, and all those are one who see it and love'.[42] It is important to appreciate that she is not describing the collapse of a person's created identity, but rather its full flowering in differentiating Union. None of this appears on a CCTV camera. Her quirks of character remain constant. Note also that while she lives outside of this flowering of unitive awareness, she is still at the height of her activity and in much need of her sharp discursive faculties for the practical (and practically impossible) tasks of founding reformed Carmelite monasteries for both women and men of her Order; negotiating the worst sorts of political scheming and plotting from the un-reformed male branch of the Carmelites, and writing to King Philip II yet again to intercede on her behalf (to say nothing of her need to adopt the rhetorical posture of a mere woman in order to escape theological censorship[43]). At the same time, she can speak out of this unitive awareness of how things are perceived from within. There are no dualisms that can cling to an authentically contemplative life. Like all pet dualisms, they are in the eyes of the dualist and always based on the lack of that inner, ocean stillness that Gregory the Theologian says is crucial to the training of the theologian.

St. Teresa's younger protégé and co-reformer in Carmel, St. John of the Cross, is keenly aware of these different epistemological stages in the life of the Christian pilgrim not simply by virtue of his scholastic education at the University of Salamanca, but also by his inner realization of the heart of Christian anthropology; in *The Living Flame of Love* he says quite simply, 'The soul's centre is God'.[44] In *The Sayings of Light and Love*, he gives us a hint of what his practice of prayer has been simplified to: 'Preserve a loving awareness of God, with no desire to feel or understand any particular thing concerning God.'[45] It is worth noting that St. John of the Cross lived this life of unitive awareness at the same time as being one of the outstanding lyric poets of Spain's Golden Age'.[46] Not only has he given us a glimpse of what his practice of prayer is like, he also says what it is like to overcome the illusion of separation from God, who is already our centre. What is it like? St. John of the Cross tells us, 'It seems to such a person ... that the entire universe is an ocean of love in which one is engulfed, for, conscious of the living centre of love within, it is unable to catch sight of the boundaries of love.'[47] St. John of the Cross is sufficiently educated in theology to distinguish between human love and divine love. But to make an intellectual distinction requires a discursive faculty of the mind, which is not a unitive faculty. In this humble blossoming of the flower of the mind, St. John of the Cross has bent to the service of unitive awareness the discursive capacities of language, only to etch the ineffable in words.

Think for a moment of that creature the sponge, which lives in the ocean. It looks within and sees nothing but ocean. All of its membrane is saturated in and porous to ocean; otherwise this sponge would not be what it is created to be, a sponge. The same sponge looks out and sees nothing but ocean. All that is within the sponge is ocean, but not all the ocean is in the sponge. When St. Gregory of Nyssa, the other Gregory, turns to comment on the Beloved Disciple lying on the Lord's breast, he uses the image of the sponge to great effect: St. Gregory of Nyssa likens the heart of the Beloved Disciple to a sponge. As St. John rests his heart 'like a sponge' on the Lord's heart, the Beloved Disciple receives 'an ineffable communication of the mysteries lying hidden in the heart of the Lord'.[48] What is the result of this heart adhering to heart and the transmissions received from the hidden places of the Lord's heart? The beloved turns around and 'tenders the breast of the Word for the nourishment of all'.[49] John, the Beloved Disciple, thus becomes John the Theologian.

When does the practice of contemplation become a way of life, a foundation for the practice of theology? When one's contemplative practice breaks through by grace into the light of contemplation and begins the process of seeing through the illusion of separation from God, an illusion sustained by a mind full of clutter, integrating our vision into the ocean vastness of God's own Word born ever anew of the Father's silence, 'a presence, then', as R. S. Thomas puts it, 'whose margins are our margins; that calls us out over our own fathoms'.[50]

Notes

1 Aristotle, *Metaphysics*, I, 980.a.21, 'Every person by nature desires to know'.
2 This poem, 'Of Theologians', is part of a longer series of poems called *On God* in R. S. Thomas, *Collected Later Poems 1988–2000* (Tarset, Northumberland, UK: Bloodaxe Books, 2004), p. 150.
3 Czeslaw Milosz, 'Treatise on Theology 4, I Apologize' in *Second Space* (New York: Harper Collins, 2004), p. 49.
4 John McGuckin, *St Gregory of Nazianzus: An Intellectual Biography* (Yonkers, NY: St. Vladimir's Seminary Press, 2001); Christopher Beeley, *Gregory Nazianzen on the Trinity and the Knowledge of God* (New York: Oxford University Press), Andrew Hoffer, *Christ in the Life and Teaching of Gregory Nazianzen* (Oxford: Oxford University Press, 2013).
5 For an excellent orientation to this problematic see Anthony Meredith, S.J., *The Cappadocians* (Yonkers, NY: St Vladimir's Seminary Press, 1987); for deeper explorations of this topic see Manlio Simonetti, *La Crisi Ariana del IV secolo* (Rome: Istituto Patristico "Augustinianum", 1975); Rowan Williams, *Arius: Heresy and Tradition*, rev. ed. (Grand Rapids, MI: Eerdmans, 2001).
6 For an in-depth study of Eunomius and his followers see the study by Richard Paul Vaggione, *Eunomius Cycicus and the Nicene Revolution* (Oxford: Oxford University Press, 2000).
7 Given the prevalence of skin diseases that plagued the body in Late Antiquity, the metaphor of 'itching' could also suggest that the Eunomian's way of going about theology is diseased and in need of healing; for an illuminating examination of the impact of disease on attitudes to the body in Late Antiquity see Margaret R. Miles, *Plotinus on Body and Beauty: Society, Philosophy, and Religion in Third Century Rome* (Oxford: Blackwell, 1999); see especially pp. 83–110.
8 *Oration* 27, 1 (p. 25). All translations of Gregory Nazianzen are taken from the easily accessible translation by Frederick Williams and Lionel Wickham, trans., *On God and Christ: The Five Theological Orations and Two Letters to Cledonius* (Yonkers, NY: St. Vladimir's Seminary Press, 2012).
9 Ibid. Theology as entertainment is the implication here.
10 Ibid.
11 Ibid., 2.
12 Ibid., 2.
13 *Oration* 27, 3 (pp. 26–27).
14 Ibid.
15 Ibid; see Ps 46 (45):10 (11).
16 Ibid; translation altered slightly.
17 Ibid., 8 (p. 30).
18 Ibid. Cf., Plotinus, *Enneads*, I.6.9, trans. Stephen Mackenna, Penguin Classics, (Harmondsworth: Penguin Books), p. 54; while Nazianzen may well have known this passage from *Ennead* I, he would likely have been exposed to contemporary theory of sculpture while studying in Athens with Basil.
19 *Oration* 28 (p. 37).
20 Palladius, *The Lausiac History*, chap. 38, trans., Robert T. Meyer, *Ancient Christian Writers 34* (Mawah, NJ: Paulist Press 1964). There are many recent and exciting studies of Evagrius. See for example, Augustine Casiday, *Reconstructing the Theology of Evagrius Ponticus: Beyond Heresy* (Cambridge UK: Cambridge University Press, 2013); Luke Dysinger, *Psalmody and Prayer in the Writings of Evagrius Ponticus* (Oxford: Oxford University Press, 2005).

21 See Evagrius, *The Praktikos*, Ch. 6., p. 16, in *The Praktikos and Chapters on Prayer*, trans. John Eudes Bamberger, Cistercian Studies Series 4 (Kalamazoo, MI: Cistercian Publications, 1981). All citations come from Bamberger's translation.

22 Evagrius, *The Praktikos*, Ch. 54 (p. 31).

23 Evagrius, *Chapters on Prayer*, Ch. 50 (p. 29).

24 See Evagrius, *The Praktikos*, Ch. 50 (pp. 29–30).

25 See John Eudes Bamberger's 'Introduction', to Evagrius, *The Praktikos*, p. lxxxii.

26 Evagrius, *The Praktikos*, Ch. 64 (pp. 33–34); translation altered slightly.

27 See Prologue 1, 5 in Evagrius, *Talking Back: A Monastic Handbook for Combating Demons*, trans., David Brakke (Trappist, KY: Cistercian Publications, 2009).

28 See *Talking Back*, for abundant examples.

29 On the possibility that Evagrius himself was taught the Jesus Prayer by his teacher, Macarius, see Antoine Guillaumont 'The Jesus Prayer among the Monks of Egypt', *The Eastern Churches Review*, 6 (1974), pp. 66–71 at p. 67.

30 St. John Climacus, *The Ladder of Divine Ascent*, Ch. 27, trans. C. Luibheid and N. Russel (Mahwah, NY: Paulist Press, 1982), p. 270; translation altered slightly. For a more extensive study of the use of the breath in Christian contemplative practice, see Martin Laird, '"Continually Breathe Jesus Christ": Stillness and Watchfulness in the *Philokalia*', *Communio* 34 (2007), pp. 243–263.

31 See Columba Stewart, 'Imageless Prayer and the Theological Vision of Evagrius Ponticus', *Journal of Early Christian Studies* 9 (2001), pp. 173–204.

32 Evagrius, *Chapters on Prayer*, Ch. 3, p. 56; translation altered slightly.

33 Ibid., Ch. 70 (p. 66); translation altered slightly.

34 Kallistos Ware, 'Prayer in Evagrius of Pontus and the Macarion Homilies' in *An Introduction to Christian Spirituality*, ed. R. Waller and B. Ward (London: SPCK, 1999), p. 16.

35 Ibid., Ch. 61 (p. 65).

36 Ibid., Ch. 34 (p. 60).

37 Ibid., Ch. 60 (p. 65).

38 St. Augustine, *Confessions*, 7, 14, trans. Benignus O'Rourke (London: Darton, Longman and Todd, 2013).

39 St. Augustine, Sermon 88.5 in *The Works of St. Augustine*, part 3, book 3, trans. Edmund Hill (Brooklyn: New City Press, 1991), p. 422; translation altered slightly.

40 St. Catherine of Genoa, *Life and Doctrine of Saint Catherine of Genoa*, chapter 14, trans. The Italian reads: '*dico dentro di me: il mio "me" egli e Dio, ne altro "me" conosco salvo ch' esso Dio mio*'. My thanks to Dr. Kevin Hughes for providing me the Italian text; see also Bernard McGinn, *The Varieties of Vernacular Mysticism* (New York: Herder, 2012), pp. 306–329), not to forget Baron von Hügel's classic study, *Mystical Elements of Religion in St. Catherine of Genoa and her Friends* (London: J. M. Dent and Sons, 1908).

41 St. Teresa of Avila, *The Interior Castle*, trans. Mirabai Starr (New York: Riverhead Books, 2003), pp. 269–270.

42 St. Augustine, *Confessions*, 10.34, trans. Henry Chadwick (Oxford: Oxford University Press, 1992), p. 209.

43 See Allison Weber, *Teresa of Avila and the Rhetoric of Femininity* (Princeton: Princeton University Press, 1996); see also Gillian Ahlgren, *Teresa of Avila and the Politics of Sanctity* (Ithaca, NY: Cornell University Press, 1996).

44 St. John of the Cross, *The Living Flame of Love*, 1, 12, in *The Collected Works of St. John of the Cross*, translated by Kieran Kavanaugh and Otillio Rodriguez, rev. ed. (Washington, DC: Institute of Carmelite Studies, 1991), p. 645.

45 St. John of the Cross, *The Sayings of Light and Love*, 88, in *The Collected Works of St. John of the Cross*, translated by Kieran Kavanaugh and Otillio Rodriguez, rev. ed. (Washington, DC: Institute of Carmelite Studies, 1991), p. 92.

46 See Colin Thompson, *Songs of the Night: St. John of the Cross* (London: SPCK, 2002).

47 St. John of the Cross, *The Living Flame of Love*, 2, 10; translation altered slightly.
48 St Gregory of Nyssa, *Homilies on the Song of Songs*, in *Gregorii Nysseni Opera*, vol. 6, ed. Werner Jäger, 41, 7–12; translation my own.
49 Ibid.
50 R. S. Thomas, 'AD', in *Collected Later Poems*, p. 118.

9   The guidance of St. Ephrem

A vision to live by

Sebastian Brock

A reader might well ask, 'what is the relevance to the topic of the Practice of the Presence of God of a writer who lived long ago and who came from a faraway country?' St. Ephrem, however, was proclaimed a 'Doctor of the universal Church', now approaching a century ago, by Pope Benedict XV (in 1920), and on these grounds alone it would seem that he is at least someone who has something of value to say to the Church in the modern world.

Who, then, is St. Ephrem? Born in the early years of the fourth century, he died the same year as St. Athanasius, in 373, when St. Augustine was in his last year as a teenager. Most of his life was spent serving as a deacon in Nisibis, in what is today south-east Turkey, on the border with Syria, but in the fourth century in the eastern-most province of the Roman Empire, on the border with the Persian Empire. The last ten years of his life were spent as a refugee, Nisibis having been handed over to Persia in the peace treaty of 363; he eventually settled in Edessa (modern Şanliurfa) whose king, Abgar V, was said to have corresponded with Jesus. Ephrem was already famous in his own day as a poet, writing in the dialect of Aramaic known as Syriac. A large body of his poems have survived.

Ephrem was not just a very fine religious poet, but at the same time he was also a profound theologian who deliberately chose to express his theological vision in poetry, rather than (as we might expect it today) in prose. Something of this vision can inspire today as much as it did in the fourth century is what I will attempt to outline here.

Ephrem's spiritual vision is not something that he himself ever describes in any single place, or at any one time; instead, it constitutes the hidden substructure of his poetry, a substructure of which readers of his poetry only gradually becomes aware as she or he grows more familiar with the poems. Ephrem's understanding of the world and its relationship to its Creator is essentially holistic and he discovers interconnections everywhere: these may be, as it were, on a horizontal plane, between everyone and everything and not just in the present, but also in the past and in the future. At the same time, the interconnections also function on a vertical plane, between denizens of the created world and their Creator, there being a sharp divide, or 'chasm' (as Ephrem terms it), between the two, over which only the Creator can cross. Thus, the interconnections are multidimensional, and at the same time, both synchronic and diachronic.

With his theological and spiritual vision, it is not so much some specific guidance on a spiritual path that Ephrem is offering us, but rather a particular mode of perception by which we can live and thereby discover deeper meaning in life. This mode of perception brings an awareness of the intricate interconnections between the material and the spiritual worlds, and between each of us as individual parts of creation and the rest of creation – both fellow human beings, and the natural world around us.

As an essential starting point for the journey of discovery, an openness of mind is required, as is the willingness to concede that there is at least a *possibility* that meaning might be found in the created world around us. With this minimal element of faith (as Ephrem would describe it) being present, the interior, or spiritual, eye is enabled dimly to see pointers to divine reality, and these pointers in turn encourage and strengthen the eye of faith so that it then becomes increasingly enabled to see these pointers to a different reality more clearly, thus proceeding, as it were, by a spiral of reciprocity: as the faith grows stronger, so does the vision of the interior eye. One might compare the process to the different ways in which one can see (or fail to see) a spider's web: the awareness that spider webs exist corresponds to the initial element of faith, but ordinarily they are invisible, or rather, simply not seen; it is only when one catches them against a particular light, or above all, when they are covered with drops of dew, that they become clearly visible.

Ephrem sees the principle of cooperation, or synergy, as being fundamental to the ways in the relationship between the God the Creator and humanity, as part of his creation: the initiative of crossing over the 'chasm' which separates creation from its Creator has first to be taken by God himself, who then provides humanity with these 'pointers' within creation, by which humans can acquire a knowledge of his hidden existence. The possibility of gaining some knowledge of God is, thus, *offered* to each individual human being: it is *not* imposed, for the individual's response will depend on the use of the gift to humanity of free-will. As Ephrem points out:

> Any kind of adornment that is the result of force
> is not genuine, for it is merely imposed.
> Herein lies the greatness of God's gift (sc. of free-will)
> that people can adorn themselves of their own accord,
> seeing that God has removed all compulsion.
> (*Nisibene Hymns*, 16:11)

What are these 'pointers' to a divine reality? Ephrem's term is the Syriac word *rāzā*, which is usually translated as 'mystery', and the plural, *rāzē*, corresponds to the Greek *ta mysteria*, 'the (Eucharistic) Mysteries', or Sacraments. Very frequently, however, in translating Ephrem's poetry it seems more helpful to employ 'symbol(s)', but with the immediate proviso that 'symbol' is to be understood, *not* in the weak modern sense of something essentially different from what is symbolized, but in the strong sense, as found in all early Christian literature, according to which the symbol is intimately – one might say, ontologically – connected with what it symbolizes: what connects symbol (*rāzā*) and what is symbolized (*shrārā*, 'divine reality', literally 'truth') is what Ephrem describes as a 'hidden power'. These *rāzē* symbols constitute the means by which God reveals himself to humanity; they are present, but latent, everywhere and at all times, to be discovered in God's two 'witnesses' (John 8:17) to his existence with which he has provided humanity, namely, 'Nature and the Book', the natural world and the Scriptures:

> Wherever you turn your eyes, there is God's rāzā/symbol,
> whatever your read, there you will find his types.
> *(Hymns on Virginity* 20:12)

In more detail:

> In his book Moses described
> the creation of the natural world,
> so that both Nature and his Book
> might testify to the Creator,
> the natural world through people's use of it,
> the Book through their reading of it.
> They are the witnesses which reach everywhere,
> they are to be found at all times,
> present at every hour,
> rebuking the unbeliever
> who denies the Creator.
> *(Hymns on Paradise* 5:2)

While the initiative of making these *rāzē*, or pointers to a knowledge of himself, has been taken by God, it remains up to each individual to exercise their free-will in deciding whether or not to make use of this possibility of acquiring a knowledge of God. Ephrem, thus, addresses Christ,

> Lord, your symbols are everywhere,
> yet you are hidden from everywhere.
> *(Hymns on Faith* 4:9)

Hidden from the physical eye, these symbols are nevertheless capable of being seen by the interior eye that has already been mentioned. This is the eye of the heart, the focal point of a person's spiritual being. According to Ephrem's understanding of optics, the physical eye sees all the better, the more it is filled by light. His interior eye functions in an analogous way, but this time it is faith, not light, which enables it to see, and so the greater the faith, the more *rāzē* does this interior eye perceive.

While it is the presence of faith, even if only a minimal amount, that is the essential starting point if the interior eye is to begin to function, there are three further elements that need to be present if the vision of the interior eye is to function properly. The first is indicated in the Beatitudes of the Gospels, 'blessed are the pure in heart, for they shall see God' (Mt 5:8). Only if the interior eye is 'pure' and unclouded by sin will it be able to perceive the *rāzē* fully and thereby come to 'see God'. A second requirement, according to Ephrem, is right belief (not dissimilar to the Buddhist requirement of 'right view'). What Ephrem has in mind here is an orthodox faith concerning Christ, as opposed to some form of 'Arian' teaching, subordinating him to the Father. This is necessary because any wrong belief would lead to a skewed vision. Finally, and in many ways most important of all, there is the need for a right attitude, which means an attitude of love. In Ephrem's own words:

> Your fountain, Lord, is hidden
> from the person who does not thirst for you;
> your treasury is empty
> to the person who rejects you.
> Love is the treasurer
> of your heavenly treasure store.
>   (*Hymns on Faith* 32:3)

Love, however, needs to be accompanied by 'Truth', by which Ephrem here means orthodox belief:

> Truth and Love are wings that cannot be separated,
> for Truth without Love is not able to fly,
> so too, Love without Truth is not able to soar up,
> for their yoke is one of harmony.
>   (*Hymns on Faith* 20:12)

In a similar vein, Ephrem ends one of his hymns in the cycle of fifteen meditative poems on the theme of Paradise:

> With Love and instruction
> commingled with Truth
> the intellect can grow
> and become rich with new things
> as it meditates with discernment
> on the treasure store of hidden symbols/mysteries (rāzē).
> For my part, I have loved, and so learned,
> and become assured
> that Paradise possesses

the haven of the victorious.
As I have been held worthy to perceive it,
so make me worthy to enter it.
                    (*Hymns on Paradise* 6:25)

The presence of 'the hidden power' in the symbols/mysteries that are latent in the created world lends a sacramental character to the natural world. Put differently, the process of the interior eye's perception becoming more and more illumined by faith leads to a sacralizing vision of the world around us, and once everything is seen as sacred, this awareness then requires that the natural world be treated with reverence and made use of with a proper sense of responsibility. Conversely, wrong action or wrong choice on the part of human beings have consequences in the natural world, as Ephrem points out, using the narrative of the Fall in Genesis 2–3 to make his point:

The sprouting of the thorn (Gen. 3:18)
testified to the novel sprouting of wrong actions,
for thorns did not sprout
as long as wrong-doing had not yet burst forth,
but once there had peered out
hidden wrong choices made by free-will,
then the visible thorns began to peer out from the earth.
                    (*Hymns on Faith* 28:9)

Elsewhere, Ephrem gives the example of Jezebel's evil action in causing the miscarriage of justice (I Kings 21) as having a repercussion in the natural world:

Because Jezebel defrauded Truth
the earth refused its produce,
the womb of the earth held back, as a reproof,
the seeds that the farmer had lent it.
                    (*Hymns on Virginity* 7:3)

Very much like the so-called 'butterfly effect' in the world of physics, human sin, in Ephrem's understanding, can have an effect on the natural world in all sorts of unexpected places.

Turning more specifically now to 'the Book', we can find much in Ephrem's approach that is both illuminating and helpful, especially in the context of any *lectio divina*. For many readers of the Bible, both ancient and modern, the anthropomorphic language of many passages in the Old Testament is a stumbling block. Ephrem has his own way of dealing with the problem by making use of the clothing imagery that came to be used in the Syriac-speaking Church to describe the Incarnation. Already in the Syriac translation of the Nicene Creed, corresponding to the Greek and Latin 'he became incarnate' (literally, 'enfleshed'), the phrase 'he put on the body' was used. With this in mind, Ephrem speaks of the Incarnation being preceded by God having 'put on names' in the Old Testament, which is, descending to a human level and allowing himself to be spoken of in human language and with terms that have nothing to do with his true nature. To illustrate what he means, Ephrem used the analogy of a human being teaching a parrot – his fellow creature – to speak by means of using a mirror:

> A person who is teaching a parrot to speak
> hides behind a mirror and teaches it in this way:
> when the bird turns in the direction of the voice speaking
> it finds in front of its eyes its own resemblance reflected;
> it imagines that it is another parrot, conversing with itself.
> The man puts the bird's image in front of it,
> so that thereby it might learn to speak.
>
> The bird is related to the man,
> but although this relationship exists, the man beguiles and teaches
> the parrot something alien to itself by means of itself;
> in this way he speaks with it.
> The Divine Being, who in all things is exalted above all things,
> in his love has bent down from on high and acquired from us our own
>   customs:
> he has laboured by every means so as to turn all to himself.
>
> $\qquad\qquad\qquad\qquad\qquad$ (*Hymns on Faith* 31:6–7)

To take the terms used about God in the biblical text literally is totally misguided; indeed,

> If someone concentrates his attention
> solely on the terms used of God's Majesty,
> he abuses and misrepresents that Majesty
> by means of those very same terms
> with which God has clothed himself for humanity's own benefit,
> and that person is ungrateful to the Grace
> which has bent down its stature to the level of human childishness.
> Even though God has nothing in common with it,
> he has clothed himself in the likeness of humanity.
>
> $\qquad\qquad\qquad\qquad\qquad$ (*Hymns on Paradise* 11:6)

Instead, in reading the biblical text,

> We should realize that, if God had not put on these terms,
> it would not have been possible for him
> to speak with us human beings. By means of what belongs to us
> he has drawn close to us:

he has clothed himself in our language so that he might clothe us
with his mode of life. He asked for our form and put this on,
and then, as a father with his children, he spoke with our childish state.

(*Hymns on Faith* 31:2)

A further point that Ephrem insists upon is the plurality of spiritual interpretations that can be found in the biblical text. Whereas in any academic approach
to the text, there is (at least in theory) only one correct historical interpretation,
from Ephrem's standpoint (which is basically that of any *lectio divina*), provided
that the biblical text is approached with his pairing of 'Truth and Love', it is
capable of yielding an infinite number of insights or meanings, each of which
will be valid for a particular individual at a particular time. In a prose work
Ephrem compares the Scriptures to an ever-flowing fountain: just as everyone
can drink from it as much as they like, yet its water is never exhausted, so too
the spiritual meanings to be found in the Scriptures are never ending:

> Anyone who encounters Scripture should not suppose that the single one
> of its riches is the only one to exist; rather, he should realize that he himself
> is only capable of discovering that one out of the many riches in it.
> (*Commentary on the Diatessaron, or Gospel Harmony*, I.18)

The two different approaches to the biblical text need to be seen to be complementary, and *not* in conflict with one another. It is only when one of the two
approaches makes claims of exclusivity, and denies the validity of the other, that
a conflict arises. Ephrem himself was well aware that these two very different
approaches existed, functioning on different planes, and he calls one 'factual'
and the other 'spiritual'. Many other early Christian writers make similar distinctions, while much later on, in the medieval West, a more detailed fourfold
categorization was developed.

In several places Ephrem describes his own experience of reading Scripture.
In one of his Hymns on Paradise, which constitute an extended meditation on
the meaning of the Paradise narrative in Genesis, he writes:

> I read the opening of this book
> and was filled with joy,
> for its verses and lines
> spread out their arms to welcome me;
> the first rushed out and kissed me,
> and led me on to its companion;
> and when I reached that verse
> wherein is written
> the story of Paradise,
> it lifted me up and transported me
> from the bosom of the book
> to the very bosom of Paradise.

The eye and the mind
travelled over the lines
as over a bridge, and entered together
the story of Paradise.
The eye as it read
transported the mind;
in return the mind, too,
gave the eye rest
from its reading,
for when the Book had been read
the eye had rest,
but the mind was engaged.

Both the bridge and the gate
of Paradise
did I find in this Book;
I crossed over and entered –
my eye indeed remained outside
but my mind entered within.
I began to wander
amid things not described.
This is a luminous height,
clear, lofty and fair:
Scripture names it Eden,
the summit of all blessings.
                    (*Hymns on Paradise* 5:3–5)

Very much in harmony with Ephrem's insistence on the multiplicity of spiritual meanings in any given passage of Scripture is his dislike of definitions, etymologically 'setting boundaries' (Latin *fines*), in areas of theology that lie beyond the 'chasm' that separates creation from the Creator. As Ephrem himself puts it,

A person who is capable of investigating
becomes the container of what he investigates;
a knowledge which is capable of containing the Omniscient
is greater than him,
for it has proved capable of measuring the whole of him.
A person who investigates the Father and So
is thus greater than them!
Far be it, then, and something anathema
that the Father and Son should be investigated
while dust and ashes exalts itself.
                    (*Hymns on Faith* 9:16)

Rather, this is the area where one can only speak in terms of paradoxes, and here it is helpful to imagine a circle, the central point of which is left unidentified, but all around the circumference are sets of paradoxes illustrating different aspects of the Hidden and the Revealed in the Godhead:

> One kind of knowledge [of God] is of what is revealed, the other of what is hidden: knowledge with respect to his revealed state, and non-knowledge with respect to his hiddenness.
>
> (*Verse Homilies on Faith*, VI, 289–92)

Ephrem has a whole range of paradoxes that serve to illustrate the mystery of the incarnation, such as 'the Exalted One who became lowly', 'the Great One who became small', 'the Rich One who became poor', and so on; it is the point at which all of these paradoxes around the circumference of the circle cross each other that 'truth' (*shrara*), or divine reality, is to be located. The multiple paradoxes then, as it were, spark off in the human mind a glimpse into what cannot ever be properly 'defined' by the human mind.

Underlying so much of Ephrem's thinking about the character of the Christian life is the idea of synergy, the interplay between what is offered by God and the response given on the part of the individual human being. In the case of Ephrem's experience reading the Paradise narrative of Genesis, it was his response, accompanied by Truth and Love, which resulted in the illumination he received. The supreme example of this synergy, or working together, of the human and the divine was of course provided by the narrative of Mary's response to the angel Gabriel in Luke's Gospel. Ephrem, in common with many other early Christian writers, contrasted Mary's 'wise' questioning of the angel with Eve's failure to question critically the serpent's misleading representation of God's words. Mary's co-operation with the Holy Spirit led to her giving birth to God the Word. In the course of the Christian life, Ephrem sees that the locus for a creative birthgiving is present in every celebration of the Eucharistic Mysteries: there the descent of the Holy Spirit upon the Bread and Wine provides a counterpart to the descent of the same Spirit upon Mary; accordingly, it is Mary, with her response, who provides a paradigm for each individual Christian, inviting a similar response to Spirit as presence, resulting in a spiritual birthgiving. Addressing Christ, Ephrem writes:

> In your Bread there is hidden the Spirit who is not consumed,
> in your Wine there dwells the Fire that is not drunk:
> the Spirit is in your Bread, the Fire in your Wine –
> a manifest wonder, that our lips have received!
>
> (*Hymns on Faith* 10:8)

And a little further on he exclaims,

> See, Fire and Spirit are in the womb of her who bore you,
> See, Fire and Spirit are in the river in which you were baptised,
> Fire and Spirit are in our baptismal font,
> in the Bread and the Cup are Fire and Holy Spirit.
>
> (*Hymns on Faith* 10:17)

Since for Ephrem the aim of the Christian life is the recovery of the divine image (Gen. 1:27), and thus becoming 'conformed' with Christ (Phil. 3:10), the encounter of the individual Christian with the Holy Spirit on receiving the Mysteries at Communion should, by implication, result in a spiritual birthgiving that consists in an ever closer conformity with Christ, so that the image of God in each individual (Gen. 1:26–7), like a polished mirror, finally clearly reflects Christ, its prototype, having cleansed away all the grime that had previously prevented the internal mirror of the soul from functioning properly:

> One complains about a mirror if its clarity is obscured
> because it has become spotted, or grime has built up,
> covering it over for those who look into it.
>
> (*Hymns on Faith* 34:4)

The refrain for this hymn is 'Blessed is he who has polished our mirror', and here one needs to recall that in antiquity a mirror was not made of glass, but of metal, and so it required constant polishing if it was to provide a clear reflection.

In another hymn Ephrem compares the Eucharist to the Wedding Feast of Cana, but now Christ is no longer the guest, but the Bridegroom. Once again addressing Christ, Ephrem says,

> here is your own pure and fair wedding feast …
> The soul is your bride, the body your bridal chamber;
> your guests are the senses and the thoughts;
> and if a single body is a wedding-feast for you,
> how great is your banquet for the whole Church!
>
> (*Hymns on Faith* 14:4–5)

Ephrem and many other Syriac writers speak of the heavenly 'Bridal Chamber' when referring to the Kingdom of Heaven. In this passage Ephrem uses the same imagery to indicate the potential intimacy of the union of love between each individual soul and Christ that is offered at each Eucharist.

Ephrem offers a wonderfully holistic way of looking at the world from a spiritual perspective, thus suggesting to us a way of finding meaning in life, of discovering the intricate network of interconnections between this world and the heavenly world and of realizing the interdependence between everyone and everything. It is a sacralizing vision, and as an important consequence, a very ecological one, which is made all the more relevant in light of his emphasis on the right use of our freewill – especially relevant when seen in the context of the 'dominion' granted to human beings over the rest of the creation in Genesis 1:28, which is very closely linked with their having been created in the image of God (Gen. 1:26–7). Ephrem emphasizes that this authority accordingly carries with it the responsibility to use our freewill in right and just ways, in order to reflect those of God, while the abuse of this God-given authority through the wrong actions carried out by our freewill will result in serious consequences in unexpected places.

He also offers us a very creative way of approaching the biblical text from a standpoint of faith: for any true *lectio divina* to bear fruit, three things are required: love, purity of heart and right belief. With the presence of these three prerequisites, the biblical text becomes like an inexhaustible fountain from which to drink. In the same passage, in which Ephrem compares the biblical text to a fountain, he points out that

> the facets of God's words are more numerous than the faces of those who learn from them. God has depicted his words with many beauties, so that each of those who learn from them can examine that aspect of them which he likes. And God has hidden within his words all sorts of treasures, so that each of us can be enriched by them from what aspects we meditate on.
>
> (*Commentary on the Diatessaron* I:18)

10 The threat of death as a test for theological authenticity

Luigi Gioia

Right from the first lines of the 1965 novel *Stoner*, its author, John Williams, unemotionally informs the reader that William Stoner was a plain and inconspicuous character: he entered the University of Missouri in 1910, he taught there until his death in 1956 and today, 'to the older ones, his name is a reminder of the end that awaits them all, and to the younger ones it is merely a sound which evokes no sense of the past and no identity with which they can associate themselves or their careers'.[1]

It is a story of endless failures: in friendship, in marriage, in the relation to his beloved daughter, in his initially invigorating love affair with one of his students, in his dealings with the inevitable and poisoning politics of academic life, in his research, in his teaching[2] – ending with death by cancer. Stoner's taciturn stoicism through such a flood of misfortunes does not confer dignity on his character but strikes us as pathetic, as a sign of weakness or of a lack of imagination. The reader, who cannot help but hope for an awakening at each turn of the story – and on a couple of occasions is even led to believe that this might happen – is increasingly frustrated with the mournful resignation of this character. For most of the book the only interest the reader can find in this story relies on the dispassionate emotional clarity of Williams's description.

All this changes, however, at the end of the novel with the account of Stoner's death. The style reaches a degree of purity that transfigures this character and his life. This death casts a retrospective light on the whole book. While not pretending to render Stoner's or any other life meaningful, this death illustrates that however long a journey towards true feeling might be, and even if this awakening occurs only at the very end of one's life for a passing second, it can still redeem a whole life.

When the reader reconsiders the whole story in the light of this death he notices that earlier in the book Stoner undergoes a death in midlife symmetrically opposed to the final one:

> He had come to that moment in his age when there occurred to him, with increasing intensity, a question of such overwhelming simplicity that he had no means to face it. He found himself wondering if his life was worth living; if it had ever been. It was a question, he suspected, that came to all

men at one time or another; he wondered if it came to them with such impersonal force as it came to him.[3]

This realization brings to him a sadness not related to particular circumstances of his life but which was all-encompassing; it also stirs a 'grim and ironic pleasure' in the futility and emptiness of that learning that had been his main consolation in life up to that moment. The scene is set during winter and the 'delicate and intricate cellular being of the snow', its whiteness on which nothing moves, is 'a dead scene which seemed to pull at him, to suck at his consciousness just as it pulled the sound from the air and buried it within a cold white softness. [...] For an instant he felt himself go out of the body that sat motionless before the window'.[4]

A sudden metallic noise brings him back to the sad reality he reluctantly finds still waiting for him; he gathers a book and a few papers and walks 'slowly home, aware of each footstep crunching with muffled loudness in the dry snow'.[5] One is struck by the violence of this experience, which pulls at him, sucks at his consciousness, happens at night, in the cold of the winter, surrounded by an eerie silence.

His physical death, at the end of his life, follows a pattern which is the exact opposite of this midlife encounter with nothingness. It takes place in summer, the bright sunlight of the afternoon presses upon his eyelids, the sky is blue, people are playing noisily outside his window: 'there was a richness and a sheen upon the leaves of the huge elm tree in his back yard; ... a thickness was in the air, a heaviness that crowded the sweet odours of grass and leaf and flower, mingling and holding them suspended'.

But, the most intriguing parallel between the two death-experiences is that they are both driven by a question. Just as the midlife death was triggered by the question 'Is life worth living?', the final death is driven by another question: 'What did you expect?':

> What did you expect? He thought again. A kind of joy came upon him, as if borne in on a summer breeze. He dimly recalled that he had been thinking of failure – as if it mattered. It seemed to him now that such thoughts were mean, unworthy of what his life had been. ... A sense of his own identity came upon him with a sudden force, and he felt the power of it. He was himself, and he knew what he had been.[6]

The connection John Williams establishes between these questions and death provides us with a very helpful insight for our topic. Perhaps rather ambitiously, this chapter intends to look at the question of authenticity regarding theological activity from the paradoxical viewpoint of death. It is a risky strategy, especially because the death we are referring to is not the pious and precarious *ars moriendi* (the art of dying)[7] which, after all, comes with a more than honourable pedigree in the history of Christian spirituality. We have chosen to look at death as a threat, as the intractable conundrum not only at the end but at the heart of our lives, which resists any attempt made to come to terms with it *and alerts us to the non-evidence of God as a mode of his presence.*

We do not know what death is. However many people we might have seen dying, we do not know what it is to die from the inside, what dying is. John Williams's novel comes to our rescue here too by offering a rare literary example of a description of death from the viewpoint of the person dying:

> He breathed again, deeply; he heard the rasping of his breath and felt the sweetness of the summer gathering in his lungs. And he felt also, with that breath he took, a shifting somewhere deep inside him, a shifting that stopped something and fixed his head so that it would not move. Then it passed, and he thought, So this is what it is like.[8]

John Williams's treatment of death is fascinating because it offers a paradigm for the challenges of self-knowledge. Deaths – and there are many deaths in our life – are the dreaded moments when we can no longer avoid facing the deep questions that we carry within us – these questions that lurk under the surface of all our endeavours and which life can brutally unleash upon us – the questions that 'suck at our consciousness'. Augustine famously lived through an analogous experience in his youth of the death of his friend, when he declares: 'I had become to myself a vast question (a *magna quaestio*).'[9]

In Williams's book, such questioning takes two forms. (1) 'Is life worth living?' – the trigger of the midlife death-experience – is a bad, a self-indulgent, a hopelessly all-encompassing, an unnecessary question: as if we had a choice, as if life existed to be 'worth it', as if it was not one of these immemorial preconditions in which our consciousness awakens for no reason at all and over which we have no say, which is there to be lived without having to justify its worth to anything or anyone. (2) 'What did you expect?' exemplifies in the novel the questioning that we have learnt to sustain, not because of resignation, but thanks to a more exact perception of the limitations of our life – thanks to a clearer perception of who we are, to a greater and more humble self-knowledge.

When St. Benedict, in the fourth chapter of his Rule, includes among the instruments of good works '*Mortem cotidie suspectam ante oculos habere,*[10] it is with the intention of bringing the monk to precisely this level of self-knowledge. He is not encouraging an *ars moriendi*, but he is warning the monk to be *suspicious* of the potentially destructive force of the wrong kind of questioning. It is significant that most English translations of the Rule completely omit the *suspectam.*[11] In the eyes of these translators it is doubtless seen as conveying a too pessimistic perception of death. And yet, it should not be omitted. In its bluntness, this *suspectam* gives voice to a concern: we must indeed be suspicious, watchful about the permanent questioning that goes on within us, interpret it, identify its real target and patiently learn how to sustain it. It is part of that learning about how to be human that lies at the heart of Benedict's schooling, built around discernment and discretion. It is about not taking refuge in spirituality or even worse in mysticism as an alibi to avoid facing oneself, to set oneself apart from the common lot of all human beings: we all must die, we are all exposed to the abyss of meaninglessness, not only regarding our achievements but also to our life in the presence of God. Is not *acedia*, after all, the illness of those who take spiritual life, relationship with God and self-knowledge seriously? No measure of progress in spiritual life is more infallible than the growth in heartfelt compassion and solidarity with sinners and unbelievers that shines sometimes in old and wise monks.

In the presence of death, a Christian is in a position no different from that of Stoner, that is, from any other human being on earth. Whether believers or not, whether self-consciously engaged in spiritual discipline or not, whether endowed with the gift of contemplative prayer or not, whether blessed with the grace of a certain experience of God or not, we are all equally and permanently exposed to the *non-evidence* of God; we spend the whole of our life, till our last breath, constantly wavering between the temptations of atheism and paganism; we are always claiming the priority of self-fulfilment at the expense of our belief; we are all fashioning a god in our own image, a god who justifies whatever we want to do, whatever pleases us, whatever affirms us. Atheism and paganism define us transcendentally as the inevitable consequences of our location in a limitless universe in which we are lost like insignificant specks of dust and in a land which grants us protection and sustenance only if we manage to bring its obscure and irrational forces under control.[12]

The threat of death becomes a test for authenticity in our theological activity by preventing us from escaping our human condition by a risky anticipation of eschatology, in which we claim for our talking *of* God, for our talking *to* God, a fullness, a meaningfulness, a totality, an ultimate character which none of these things can possess in this life. Or, by that other even more pernicious anticipation of eschatology whereby we claim for our *experience* of God an evidence, a priority over the never fulfilled labour of knowledge, a claim which has led to more than one ideological misuse of Christianity.

These considerations are not intended to deny the possibility of knowing God, of doing theology, of speaking meaningfully of God, of being granted an experience of God in prayer, of mysticism. They are only trying to clarify *what we must not overlook with regards to our human condition, to our humanity, if we want to have access to some authenticity in prayer, in theological activity and in life.*

Such clarification is possible, to some degree at least, both at a transcendental and at a theological level, even though, in fact, we can decipher the former only in the light of the latter. From a theological viewpoint, all hinges on the right appreciation of the secularity of the forms taken by God's revelation. God's self-revelation does not reach us otherwise than through creaturely realities which are not God. Not only are these creaturely realities not God, they are part of a fallen world which is, at least, resistant to God, and is more often hostile to him. Even from a Christological viewpoint, the humanity of Christ itself is not revelatory as such; for most of those who lived with Christ his divine identity was entirely hidden. A Christian does not see more than a non-Christian, but he is granted by some mystery the ability to trust Christ and to follow him in darkness. This secularity is not accidental or provisional, but is an inalienable attribute of the Word of God.[13]

We can never dispense ourselves from such secularity. The temptation to think that we can overlook this unsettling mediation can be a danger in some forms of mysticism, i.e. hoping that we might reach a level of knowledge of God, a level of evidence in our experience of God, which would set us apart from the rest of humanity. All attempts to see the face of God lead us either to faith or mislead us into delusion. The authenticity of spirituality can be measured only by a growing awareness of our unbelief and of our idolatry; by an even deeper compassion for those who are indifferent to God; by the awareness of our inescapable complicity with those who manipulate the divine to their advantage, with those who are incapable of believing, with those who are crushed under the weight of God's absence, with those whose 'prayer seems lost in desert ways', whose 'hymn in the vast desert dies'.[14]

What becomes, then, of theological activity? If the threat of death is inescapable, i.e. if we as Christians are just as threatened as anyone else by the great question, the *magna quaestio* of death; if we as Christians are just as exposed to the non-evidence of God, to the temptation of idolatry; if there is no way around the secularity of the means through which God makes himself known: then what chances do we have to do authentic theology, i.e. to say anything relevant or meaningful about God?

The answer could very well be that *there are no chances*, which is impossible, and we would not be mistaken. However, by grace, we have to testify that God's love has decided to overcome this impossibility and to make himself known to us in and through his Trinitarian relationship, which he extends to us, into which he introduces us.

Fides ex auditu, 'faith comes from hearing': not in the form of a past event, but of an ever actual event. Theological activity, just like the proclamation of the Word of God, rests on a relationship with God. There can be an agreement between what we say and what God says, between our knowledge of God and God's revelation, but it is never reached once for all, it can never be taken for granted, it is always an event, and thus calls for constant verification. There lies the difference between ecclesial proclamation of the Word and theological activity, the role of the latter in the service of the former.[15]

The agreement between the Word of God understood as *God-in-the-act-of-speaking* and the mission of preaching entrusted to the Church calls for constant verification, for constant critical investigation. And this is the role of theological activity. But this critical role of theological activity is based in turn on an actual and living relation with God: it requires the application of human means and competences,[16] but is made possible only in and through faith. In other words, the *fides quae*, the truths we believe in, receive their form from the *fides qua*, namely adhesion (of both love and intelligence) to God, from an actual living relation with God. This is where authenticity becomes a challenge in theological activity.

Theological activity is constantly threatened, even more so than preaching, with becoming self-reliant, with understanding its critical role regarding God's knowledge independently from the event of his revelation. Such self-reliance has found a valuable ally in the subject, the I contrived by modernity, who pretends to be neutral, to be the measurer, arbiter and even the creator of truth and values – with the paradoxical result of dehumanizing theological activity by denying its vulnerability and its responsibility.

Thus, because the event of the correspondence between God's word and human word can never be taken for granted, and because a denial of our humanity is a constant temptation, theological activity must never tire of striving for authenticity. And nothing alerts us more to the need for this authenticity than precisely a keen sense of this vulnerability, of the precariousness of all of our endeavours, of their limitations ('What did you expect?') which we have patiently learnt to sustain and somehow even to cherish. It is precisely this vulnerability that calls for a relation, which invokes God before speaking of God, which erupts into a *confession* which combines, inseparably, the acknowledgement of our sins, praise ('talking *to* God') and belief.

But, this also alerts us to what Henri de Lubac masterfully showed in his work on Origen's theological activity. In terms of patristic exegesis, theological activity consists in passing from the literal to the spiritual sense of Scripture – but 'as long as we do not turn to the Lord, the veil shall not be removed from our eyes. The passage from the letter to the spirit is the same movement of *metanoia*, of conversion'.[17]

Authenticity in theology is above all a matter of acknowledgment. To do theology, we have to let ourselves be *addressed* by the Word of God, by the Lord in the act of speaking through his Word, *and experience this event in all its different forms*: we need to encounter God's consolation, to receive God's blessing, to endure God's warnings, to answer God's summoning, to welcome God's promise, to marvel at God's plan for us, etc. But authenticity entails still more, and here the link with the threat of death might again come in handy.

In all good conscience, we can forgo the embarrassment of trying to grapple with the partly artificial construct of what we call 'post-modernism' and deal directly with what underpins it, which is nihilism. Once Kant established that ethics must be based on will and freedom, Nietzsche ends modernity and inaugurates whatever comes after it by affirming that freedom is not a property which can be attributed ahistorically and essentially to a human subject, but depends entirely on strategies of power whereby it becomes arbitrary. Hence, the duty to devote oneself to a deconstruction of all pretensions to truth through unmasking their inescapably regional character and their manipulative function, wholly instrumental to achieving or maintaining power. The consequent denial, not only of truth as such but also of the objectivity of any value, is the logical consequence of this move, which paves the way to the *Übermensch* as creator of values.[18] What survives is the will to power, which is the art of creating new values. And this means that truth is transformed into an aesthetic question: the truth is that which I like and which I can always dislike at some later stage in time. It is no longer words that express the truth that matters, but words that move me.[19]

Hence, the pervasiveness of conversations, i.e. the polite exchange of views between people with no wish to persuade one another of the truthfulness of what they feel entitled to affirm. Hence, the social predominance of consensus, made possible by the unwillingness to take any question too seriously. God himself becomes a subject of conversation, faith and ethics a matter of consensus, and this is why we soon find talking about religion much more comfortable than talking about God.[20]

In this context, therefore, to the vulnerability of theological activity outlined earlier, we would have to add the struggle to express meaning at all, to believe in the possibility of a language still capable of communicating meaning and identity beyond the realm of cultural representations *as* representations (or *as* practices). Are there still – we wonder – words, is there still a speech able to survive nihilism and even to overcome it?[21] What chance do we have of escaping this crippling moral and spiritual burden?

In line with what we have been arguing in this chapter, the sad or maybe reassuring truth is that we cannot escape it. We said that the non-evidence of God and the temptation of idolatry condition us transcendentally. But our tendency to doubt any truth, our awareness of the link between truth and power and our tendency towards an aesthetical approach to truth: these factors might not have a transcendental status, but they have undeniably come to condition or rather to 'pre-condition' us in one way or the other, at one level or another. They have become an integral part of the way we relate to issues of truth and values. And the chances are that we are not prepared to go back on this. The chances are that we do not consider our present situation worse than the time when each truth was uniformly enforced by an unquestioned and unquestionable (indeed often arbitrary) principle of authority. A time when history and difference – and therefore freedom – were not seen as constitutive of being.

The chances are that it might be too late to go back on this. We do not yield to nihilism by choice any more, we belong to it through our culture, we are born into it. We might regret it, but at some level we are all secretly or unwittingly relieved that its work is done and that there is no way back.

And yet we know that we cannot give up the hope of speaking truthfully and meaningfully either – and this is what we actually do during most of our daily life: a world, a life in which absolutely every assertion, every word would be questionable and questioned, every value would be subject to refutation, is impossible – it would deny the intrinsic sociability of human beings, their reliance on each other and therefore their responsibility to each other to exist and to perform whatever they are called to perform.

Thus, we are left with a conundrum, a *magna quaestio*.

We cannot escape the non-evidence of God, nor can we break free from our idolatrous tendencies and our individualized and disillusioned cynical self; we cannot take flight from the violence of history and our complicity with the structures of sin, nor from our anxiety with regards to time – the list goes on.

We cannot escape all this, but we might discover that we are offered – never once and for all, but for the time and the space of a relation, of an act, of an event – the possibility of not being conditioned exclusively by our humanity, the possibility of being not only citizens of the earthly city, but also, albeit symbolically, members of the city of God.

Christian life, acting and thinking consist in this tension, in this impossibility made possible, in this paradox. Indeed, is this not embedded in our constant dealings with the secularity of God's revelation we talked about earlier? Are we not those who find happiness in things we do not see? Are we not those whose defining feature, in the NT, is *hypomoné*, perseverance, in spite of the experience of God's silence and absence? Are we not those whose faith relies on the *memorial* of Christ's love for us, of God's faithfulness to us? Are we not those who keep breaking the bread throughout the centuries in memory of him who let his body to be broken to grant us life? Are we not those who take God at his word and believe it to be true – that is, truthful and faithful? Are we not those who can call God Father?

In a word, are we not, as Christians, those who, living by faith, can praise even an absent God because memory authorizes us to do so? This is because, liturgically, we embody a human chain, a church, which throughout the centuries keeps being summoned, consoled, sustained and led by the living Word of God against all odds?[22]

We can live in God's presence not as creators of new values, but simply by accepting that the threat of death, that the non-evidence of God, that the secularity of his revelation are all integral to the pre-eschatological nature of our present time and that even boredom in prayer, even the deep frustration caused by the limitations of our churches, even the constant sense of unfulfilment that characterizes our life until its very end can be the medium of a relation with God, can be sustained meaningfully – and actually are probably the means we need to keep us awake, alert, discerning and waiting.

For too long metaphysics has given us the illusion of a *tota ac simul possessio* by locating the continuity of our being, of our 'I' in the notion of substance.[23] The truth is that our self-perception is historically constituted and that it cannot account for the whole of our existence. Here too, the pre-eschatological character of our life prevents any experience from being able to capture the whole of our existence – not even the experience of death. We dream about dying like Bede who breathes his last breath only after he has dictated the last word of his book, thus completing his work.

Even here Stoner's death can help us to discern a more authentic, a more human version of reality. As his last questioning ('What did you expect?') gives way to 'a kind of joy' and to 'a sense of his own identity', Stoner reaches out to his bedside table and pulls from the jumble on the table top the one – mediocre – book he had written many years earlier:

It hardly mattered to him that the book was forgotten and that it served no use; and the question of its worth at any time seemed almost trivial. He did not have the illusion that he would find himself there, in that fading print; and yet, he knew, a small part of him that he could not deny was there, and would be there.[24]

But, as he opens the book 'it became not his own', 'he could not see what was written there'. And this is the moment he dies: '*The fingers loosened, and the book they had held moved slowly and then swiftly across the still body and fell into the silence of the room*'.[25]

No justification for such remarkable freedom in death is given by the author of the book, but we might venture an explanation. At this time of truth, Stoner perceives in all clarity the discrepancy existing between the life he is aware of, with his failures and the modest achievement of his book, and his existence. In the end, death is a threat only if our existence is coextensive with the life we are aware of (our 'consciousness').[26] If this was the case, death would indeed correspond to the deeply frustrating question 'Was it worth it?' But if this is not the case, if our existence exceeds our consciousness, then we know that there cannot be a last word,[27] and that fulfilment does not belong to life – and we can thus face the question 'What did you expect?' in all peace.

Theology authorizes us to praise Stoner's life and death even though it does not contain any explicit reference to God and to eschatology. Theology even has an interest in learning from such modesty if it is to speak to God and about God with meaning and authenticity, if it aims at all at being and remaining faithful to what it means to be human.

Notes

1 John Williams, *Stoner* (New York: New York Review Books, 2003), pp. 3f.
2 Ibid., pp. 264f.
3 Ibid., p. 179.
4 Ibid., p. 180.
5 Ibid., p. 180.
6 Ibid., p. 277.
7 Jean-Yves Lacoste, *Expérience et absolu: questions disputées sur l'humanité de l'homme* (Paris: Presses Universitaires de France, 1994), p. 204.
8 Williams, *Stoner*, p. 276.
9 Augustine, *Confessions* 4.iv.9.
10 Benedict, *Rule* 4.47. See the translation by Timothy Fry, O.S.B: 'Day by day remind yourself that you are going to die.' (translation supplied by editor) *The Rule of Benedict in Latin and English with Notes* (Collegeville, MN: The Liturgical Press, 1981).
11 Cf. for example the 1931 translation, edited by W. K. Lowther Clarke and the 1949 translation by Boniface Verheyen.
12 Cf. Lacoste, *Expérience et absolu*, pp. 7–27.
13 Karl Barth, *Church Dogmatics* (Edinburgh: T & T Clark, 1980), I.1, pp. 165–169.
14 Gerard Manley Hopkins, '*Nondum*', in *Gerard Manley Hopkins: The Major Works*, ed. Catherine Phillips (Oxford: Oxford University Press, 2009), pp. 81–82.
15 Barth, *Church Dogmatics* I.1, 72–84 and 268–274.
16 Ibid., I.1 21.

17 Henri de Lubac, *Histoire et esprit: l'intelligence de l'Écriture d'après Origène* (Paris: Aubier, 1950), p. 316.
18 Cf. John Milbank, *Theology and Social Theory: Beyond Secular Reason* (Cambridge, MA: Blackwell, 1991), pp. 279–288.
19 Jean-Yves Lacoste, *Recherches sur la parole*, Lectiones Vagagginianae (unpublished), D 26.
20 Ibid., D 30, 37.
21 Cf. ibid., D 1.
22 Ibid., D 35–38.
23 Cf. Jean-Yves Lacoste, *La phénoménalité de Dieu: neuf etudes* (Paris: Éditions du Cerf, 2008), p. 183.
24 Williams, *Stoner*, p. 277.
25 Ibid., p. 278.
26 Cf. Lacoste, *La phénoménalité de Dieu*, p. 196.
27 Ibid., p. 198.

Index

References to endnotes consist of the page number followed by the letter 'n' followed by the number of the note, e.g. 28n19 refers to note no. 19 on page 28.